WEEDING THE GARDEN OF SURRENDER

ALSO BY BELA GARY

The Midlife Crisis of a Perfect Woman
The Misadventures of an Imperfect Woman

Weeding the Garden of Surrender

Musings on Life, Love, and Letting Go

Bela Gary

Weeding the Garden of Surrender: Musings on Life, Love, and Letting Go
Copyright © 2024 by Bela Gary. All rights reserved.

Although this publication is designed to provide accurate information in regard to the subject matter covered, the publisher and the author assume no responsibility for errors, inaccuracies, omissions, or any other inconsistencies herein. This publication is meant as a source of valuable information for the reader, however, it is not meant as a replacement for direct expert assistance. If such level of assistance is required, the services of a competent professional should be sought.

Unless otherwise indicated, all the characters in this book are fictitious. Any resemblance to actual persons, living or dead, is purely coincidental.

No part of this book may be used or reproduced in any manner whatsoever without written permission, except in the case of brief quotations embodied in critical articles or reviews. For more information, email all inquiries to info@stardustings.com.

Published by Stardustings Press
PO Box 462
Hillsborough, NC 27278

www.stardustings.com

Printed in the United States of America

First Edition

ISBN: 978-1-7363797-3-8
LCCN: 2024938571

To my love, Kurt.
Your unexpected arrival is proof
of the magic and beauty of surrender.

BEGINNINGS

Let go, surrender, and forever be free.

WHY ME?

At some pivotal moment in our lives, in the face of insurmountable pain, frustration, or anger, we have all asked—*why did this happen to me?* More often than not, we question the negative, the terrible news, the deep pain. Why would we question the good, the magical, the beautiful occurrences that texture our lives?

As I moved through the process of my pain and ultimate healing, I sought advice and support from many outlets, searching for answers to existential questions, most of them unanswerable. *Why did this happen to me? Why is the pain so deep? Why is it so difficult to heal?*

We ask ourselves unceasing *whys* when something goes wrong, but most of us don't wonder *why* when something goes right. Our daily lives are filled with small, beautiful moments that we often don't appreciate enough. *How am I so blessed?* Are we grateful enough? Sometimes. We may question those moments of immense, unexpected beauty. We feel deep gratitude. The daily small moments of joy—the smell of a cup of coffee or a spectacular sunset—perhaps we don't appreciate them enough. Some of us are more likely to focus on the frustrations, the small daily annoyances. And then at times, when the more significant events happen, we are more likely to wallow in our terrible pain. We raise our hands toward the sky in desperation, openly challenging the Divine, and ask, *why did this happen to me?* We rarely raise our hands in gratitude. Why would we, if everything is beautiful? We seek to resolve our pain. It's just too much.

Like you, I searched for solutions in many places—books, blogs, websites, workshops. Scouring the internet for answers that seemed beyond my grasp.

I was soon overwhelmed. I realized I could literally spend the rest of my life digesting all the information about pain, heartbreak, and healing. A multitude of healers, therapists, spiritual guides, and so-called experts, offering contradictory advice on "how to" recover from the pain of heartbreak and grief. Psychology, spirituality, friendly advice from friends and family, trashy magazines, as well as my own ingrained beliefs, created constant circular arguments in my mind. Too much information. They all sounded helpful, offering insightful and unique perspectives. But how to choose what advice to follow? What makes one piece of proclaimed knowledge or advice accurate and another opinion wrong? Which would heal me completely so that I could erase the pain? That became my quest.

The self-help industry is inundated with sources for healing. You can fix anything from bad eating habits to childhood trauma by reading a book. There are over 45,000 self-help books published every year, each with unique ideas and proprietary methods for recovery. Books that focus specifically on heartbreak or relationships are likely a large chunk of those 45,000 books. With so many options, how does one choose the "right" book? Just because a book is popular doesn't mean it works for everyone. Maybe the author is a celebrity. Maybe it was endorsed by a celebrity. Do celebrities really know more than we do about emotional healing? Book sales or rankings don't mean anything. There could be an obscure book by an unknown author that may never make its way to the best-seller list. Popularity is often about money making and most books are published and heavily marketed by the largest publishing companies, who hope to turn a big profit. While there is nothing wrong with making money, the large publishers dominate the market and thus they decide which books are worthy of publication. Most of these books are filled with the same old ideas, reworked and regurgitated to seem shiny and new. If the genre or topic isn't a money maker, they have no interest in publishing your book.

Sometimes books break the mold and reach readers with powerful and insightful words. They make an impact. *The Power of Now*, *The Four Agreements*, and *The Untethered Soul* are some of my favorites. There are so many different books available it can be overwhelming to decide what to read. There is no one-size-fits-all—we know there is no one book that will help every single person. Again, popularity is not the best indicator. Just because a book has sold a million copies, doesn't mean it will work for you. We are all unique and all learn and thrive in different ways. What works for me may not work for you. And no single "healer" has all the answers.

I dove into reading as many books as possible, signed up for seminars and workshops, and joined countless grief groups. I digested every word in every book. I read blogs and watched videos. I tried conventional and spiritual therapy. It was all trial and error, as most of the methods and ideas just didn't seem to work for me. It was taking too long, and I was ready to leap forward. I wondered if maybe there was something wrong with me—that I couldn't be fixed. I was irreparably broken. The stack of books on my nightstand was proof of that—I felt exactly the same as I had fifty books ago.

I did make progress, eventually. As I experimented, I learned that there were bits and pieces of helpful information and certain ideas did work for me. I didn't fully encompass any one process or guidebook. This is when I began to piece together everything that resonated and worked for me. I created my own unique, individual healing plan. Eventually, I created healing plans for my clients.

That's the key. That's the answer to the endless search for healing after deep heartbreak, grief, or pain: Creating a healing plan that encompasses everything that you discover works for *you*. The big problem, because of all of the information out there, is that it may take you a very long time to find what works—as it did for me. This is the process of healing. Through learning what works for you, you open the door to self-discovery.

This book is a collection of personal essays—musings, as I call them—about healing. Some are random thoughts, and some act as guideposts to help you along your journey. For me, writing was my key to healing. It could be your key. Pain, fear, life, love—there's always something new to explore. Through writing, you open the connection to your heart and soul, and eventually, through contemplative processes, bring yourself back into balance. While the primary focus when I started this book was on the pain caused by heartbreak in romance, I soon realized that the pain I felt was tied to many of the fears I was unwilling to face. Many of my stories and writings can be applied to any difficult experience in life. This is my experience, my journey, that started with a broken heart and ended in a heart full of love.

I can't make any guarantees. This is your journey and you are the master of your healing. You must have the desire and willingness to heal, the courage to face your fears, and the strength to accept your imperfections. Write. Read. Choose what resonates. *Healing is personal, and what works for one person will not work for another.*

The ultimate goal of all healing—surrender. Living life in the moment, letting go of control. Easier said than done. But as I always tell people, if I, the ultimate fearful, pained, control freak can do it, so can you.

THE UNKEMPT GARDEN

*We're in darkness, trapped in an unkempt garden,
surrounded by nothing but pestilent weeds.*

WHY IS IRRELEVANT

Things happen. Bad things happen to good people. If life gives you lemons…you know the rest. Clichés and quotes. How I love quotes! But yes, some phrases are definitely overused and trite. They do get the point across pretty accurately sometimes. That's why they're so popular. Famous. Infamous really.

There are moments in our lives when terrible things happen, and they affect us so deeply that we go into shock. Deeply traumatizing events: death of a loved one, loss of a job, a health crisis. Even those things that some consider trivial or unimportant can affect us deeply. A small event for one can be a painful, life-changing event for another. It's in these moments that we ask—*why*? Perhaps we feel our lives were blessed. That nothing bad could ever happen to us. We are on such a clear path at a defined moment in time, we are shocked when something blows up the road in front of us. The way forward is destroyed. What was once so certain is now completely erased. A big black hole looms ahead.

We run and grab whatever random tools we can find to fill the hole so we can keep going. Sometimes, unable to find any tools, in desperation, we use our bare hands. All the while, tears stream down our faces, soaking into the new earth that we pack down. We do the best we can with what we have. We step over the newly filled hole, moving forward toward something new—never wondering about the meaning of the hole.

As we walk, the weeds grow quickly and silently around us. We don't move fast enough. The weeds begin to block our view, hinder our forward movement, and eventually they grow so dense, like a thicket, that we can no longer pass. Everything grows around us, we are confined, and the nurturing sunlight is blocked. We're in darkness, trapped in an unkempt garden, surrounded by nothing but pestilent weeds. We try to pull the weeds, but soon we discover the roots run too deep. We can no longer effectively use our bare hands.

We ask again—*why*? As humans, we desire explanations. We feel we need explanations. We've been searching for answers since the beginning of consciousness—whenever that was, however many eons ago. We have questioned our emergence and the significance of our existence. Very deep, philosophical, spiritual questions.

Questions without answers. We ponder, we contemplate. The weeds continue to grow around us.

What if I told you that you already have the answers, you have the power to plow the thicket, to pull the weeds? Just like Dorothy in The *Wizard of Oz*, you've had the power all along.

What does it take?

Surrender.

Forget the why. It's not in your control. The only thing you can control is yourself—your thoughts, your words, and your actions. Everything else is an illusion.

THE ILLUSION

Humanity has reached a point in existence where we think we have control over everything. We can heal our bodies with medicine. We can heal our minds with therapy (and sometimes medicine). We can fix world disputes with negotiations, roundtables, and bombs. We can feed the world with words and images. We make things better. More technology, more development. More chemicals in our food. Medicines and supplements to make us live longer and look younger, be as beautiful as the celebrities and models we see in the media.

But what happens to the soul?

It becomes lost in the unkempt garden, surrounded by those weeds the world once thought would save us all. The medicines, potions and lotions, chemical concoctions that we hope will give us immortality. The belief that technology will save us. AI, ChatGPT, the fake gods and prophets of a truly messed-up society. We want answers! And they must be found in the physical world. Meanwhile, the weeds have grown so high and thick, we can't take another step. We can't see. Even sound is blocked. We feel terror and pain, and then eventually, numbness, as we block out even the negative things. *Better to be numb.* Watch some mindless streaming show about aliens or monsters or something dark and sinister that may or may not eventually be exterminated by some teenagers or superheroes.

We are disconnected from our souls.

What if the world we're living in right now isn't real? What if everything we've ever done in our lives didn't matter? What if all the pain and sorrow we have ever felt isn't reality? Maybe it's a matrix, maybe our bodies are somewhere else, and our consciousness is experiencing what we call reality right now. Are we prisoners or is it by choice? We could be dreaming. The real world is a dream and our dream world is actually reality. I don't think we know what reality is. Another person's reality might look entirely different. Yellow is red and three is four. The meaning of words is meaningless because they don't exist. This reality we are living in right now is not real. We are not real. We are just souls living a human experience, an organic computer program that loves to plant weeds everywhere in our path to prevent us from attaining enlightenment. We are prisoners.

It could be true. Just like many believe in gods and God, we can believe in anything. Anything and everything is possible.

RELIGION OF SCIENCE

What was once magic is now science. Look at human history. Galileo was thought crazy and was imprisoned. Even Einstein's theories were ridiculed at one point. Copernicus. Barry Marshall. George Zweig. Google them if you don't know who they are. They were laughed at, persecuted, and blacklisted. Eventually scientific study proved their theories to be true. This is why I believe many of the "magical" aspects of existence will be proven one day. Energy healing is based on quantum physics. I know it intuitively, even though I can't explain it scientifically. It's complex, but I know one day someone will be able to explain how the particles of energy can actually be controlled and heal not only the human body, but also the parts of the soul that are stuck in this 3D reality and in need of rising to a higher dimension. I can't prove it. I just believe it.

Energy healing is a powerful method of balancing your emotions. I am a healer and have also experienced the power of healing by others. It works. Healers understand how to work with the energy that surrounds us. While some have a mystical explanation for this energy transfer, I believe that healers can manipulate the energy and extract negative frequencies that cause emotional and physical pain. Sometimes the physical and emotional are intertwined. I know one day, most of this will be explained in quantum mechanics. For now, it's a mystery, but it truly does work to bring balance to many people.

Scientists laugh at those who believe in things that can't be proven by the "scientific method." It's a matter of faith. Faith in something larger than yourself, faith in your own ability to heal yourself, faith in things that seem insane. Science laughs—and sometimes refuses to do any studies that could prove the existence of things that seem impossible. Energy healing—have there been any studies done in this area? At least some "qualified" ones? Many have attempted to study "paranormal" and "metaphysical" events. But most of these things cannot be measured by human techniques. Maybe one day, we will wake up and discover that science had it all wrong.

Science was invented. Science has rules and a methodology. Science has as much dogma as religion. If you don't believe the dogma, you are outside "normalcy." You are a conspiracy theorist. A rebel, delusional, perhaps even insane. *Science, can you prove that you are true?* You show us tests and hypotheses and the scientific method that you made up to prove your existence. Science is proven by science. A circular argument by those who are perhaps afraid to understand the truth. And while yes, I agree, science does explain quite a bit, it cannot explain the mystical and magical. It simply dismisses it. Much easier to ignore something you don't understand. Or something that might bring your whole religion crashing down. Could be a conspiracy, maybe. Some say it is. Sometimes things feel off, and I don't trust them. I do believe others feel the same way but are afraid to express that. You have to trust your gut. And I do believe your gut will tell you what's true, then you must pick and choose what to believe so you don't go in blindly. There are no rules when it comes to faith and belief. We all can intuitively sense what is right and wrong, what is truth and fiction, and what is reality and dreams.

Science has also been wrong, as we know. What was once science is now...irrelevant. At least to scientists. "We know more now than ever before." While that may be true, there's still a lot we don't know. Pharmaceuticals that were supposed to heal caused injury and were taken off the market. Cures, such as leeching or bloodletting, which were once common methods used to supposedly help people, have been disproven.

Alternative medicine, interestingly called "alternative," is already presumed to be different and not acceptable to traditional Western medicine. Alternative means those that are not "standard" to traditional medicine. However, at one point, they were commonly used and they were successful. Energy healing, herbs, and natural remedies that are less likely to harm the body. We don't need any more chemicals or diagnostic tests, infusing us with radiation and poisons, our bodies sickened, and future generations affected by mutations in our DNA.

FEAR OF QUESTIONING

Most are fearful to question. We would rather keep things status quo. Safely protected by society's views. We don't want to be outcasts. We want to fit in. We don't want to be seen as anti-social or different. If the government or the media tells us what is true, we must believe and obey.

What is wrong with questioning everything? It doesn't mean you believe something one way or another or that you don't agree. I've always and will always question everything, especially if it feels wrong in my gut. I will examine it, look at both sides, then sense the meaning before I make any judgment. And sometimes, we may never figure it out. It just is and we don't know why or what it means. We have to accept that. But I don't blindly follow what anyone says. I will question everything and examine it before I deem it to be a lie or conspiracy theory. Just like science, there have been plenty of conspiracy theories that we considered outlandish but have been proven true. We don't know, as individuals, what is really happening in the world. Again, we need to put our trust in ourselves and our intuition. That is the only way. Let them call you crazy. Let them label you whatever they want. *As long as you know the truth*. Whether it is ever revealed doesn't matter in the long run. And we shouldn't even dwell on it. Those who can't see the truth will never understand. There is just too much fear involved in knowing, and they would rather remain blind. And it's likely you can't convince anyone or change their viewpoint anyway. Go about your business and work on yourself and how you can spread love in the world. What matters most is the energy of love. The truth becomes irrelevant.

CORRUPTION OF SPIRITUALITY

Spirituality is about kindness, compassion, and love. Towards others and ourselves. That's my definition. I don't believe in the dogma of religion or science. Dogma corrupts and defeats the purpose of kindness, compassion, and love in many ways. I respect others' opinions though. I do respect those who choose to create their own definitions and follow their own truths, without fear of judgment. I don't believe in a Christian hell, but I respect your feelings and opinions that define your belief in it. As long as there are those three words—kindness, compassion, and love—and you live your life defined by those words, you are an authentic soul. Those who espouse hate or justify acts based on religious dogma, there is no love in that, and you are living an inauthentic life, full of hate and pain. That's where religion has been corrupted—by those who desire power, who persecute others for their beliefs, and who feel so uncomfortable with the different opinions of others that they feel they must destroy them. Wars have been started because of those differences and the unwillingness to accept others' viewpoints. Genocides have occurred. Torture, economic devastation, and the destruction of Mother Earth.

Spirituality is supposed to be different. It is supposed to be about acceptance and love and having faith in something larger than us—without having to follow strict "rules" that may or may not define whether you are "saved." If you treat others and our planet with kindness, you are saved already. You don't need to pray all day or obey the religious leaders.

However, spirituality has been corrupted in many ways. Spirituality has become a religion, with its own dogma and rules. Some sell programs that supposedly "teach" you how to be more spiritual. Self-proclaimed gurus, claiming they have the answers to spiritual questions. *Buy the books, buy the programs, follow the rules, and you will become enlightened*, they claim. They can heal you for several thousand dollars.

Healing is a life-long process. We are never truly healed—there is always something right around the corner we need to deal with as we move through life in the physical world. Our souls crave learning and change. But we don't need to pay out thousands of dollars nor follow any gurus or special programs to find healing, and ultimately—growth.

We don't need to pay others to heal us spiritually. Instead, we should pay others to teach us how to heal ourselves. Everyone can heal themselves. That should be the goal of every energy healer—to teach the broken, the suffering, how to heal themselves. You don't need a certificate, nor do you need endless classes. I'm a firm believer in teaching instead of continually making people believe they must invest heavily in a healer to fix them. Maybe you need some "retuning" every once in a while. Pay someone for a reiki session, sound therapy, or whatever benefits you. I do that myself. But if these healers aren't teaching you how to harness the energy around you so you can help yourself, they are not doing their job. It's simple. Learn how to harness the energy that exists around you, your energy, and then apply it.

Then there is the belief that you must get certified for everything. If you're not, you aren't credible. Someone once told me that healers shouldn't be out there practicing on clients until they are certified in their healing modalities. We don't need those certificates. I asked, *How do you know those with certificates and those who teach are qualified? How do you know they are working for the higher good of everyone?* You don't. There are many false healers out there, false prophets, those who tell you they can read the future, tell you your fortune, and predict what will happen. A Reiki Master title doesn't require a certificate or special classes, except in a society that focuses on monetizing abilities we all possess. We are all gifted and have the potential to work with energy. You have a gift and may need a bit of training, but you certainly don't need to be certified to use your gift. That was all invented for people to make money. Spirituality has become all about making money—*how can I make money teaching people how to be spiritual?*

We are all spiritual beings, and maybe we need a little guidance, but we certainly don't need to spend thousands of dollars to reach enlightenment. It's already within.

DEFINE YOUR SPIRITUALITY

The definition of spirituality is individual. What you practice, what you feel, what you believe. I try to respect all definitions.

It means finding a deeper inner connection to yourself through your practice. Meditation, prayer, and connecting to the beautiful energies that are everywhere around us.

It means having faith in something larger than yourself. Whatever label you assign, doesn't matter. God, the Universe, Source, Light, Energy, the Divine, your higher self. When you believe in something transcendent, a beautiful light that encompasses us all, you break from the chaos of the world, the hate, the war—with faith, you move toward surrender.

Why is faith important? You can have faith in yourself, but still feel alone. Everything is more difficult, and while it's admirable that you can achieve all you want and go through challenges with strength and perseverance, you are still disconnected from the universal energy. You become wrapped up in the material, wanting more things, wanting more attention. *Faith heals.* You can't heal those deep spiritual wounds without going inward, and going inward requires a certain belief in the mystical to heal your spiritual wounds. You can go to a conventional therapist for help, but there are spiritual wounds that remain that a conventional therapist may not understand. You can call it a crisis of faith. An existential crisis.

Faith in something larger than yourself brings a sense of peace. You can shed those beliefs that you have control over everything (which keeps you in frustration and anger), that there is no purpose to life (which keeps you stuck in materialism), and that we are here simply to live and die (thus we are simply biological beings without a soul).

Faith also gives you a sense of connectedness. A community. If you are just living for yourself, who exactly are you helping? Whom do you serve? Only yourself? Can you be of service to others? That is part of the problem in our world right now. But it's changing. I'm always an optimist.

Spirituality is about growth and healing.

Spirituality is also about emulating kindness, compassion, and love. *Without judgment.* Everyone is broken in their own way. Everyone is beautiful in their own way. The things we believe have been ingrained in our hearts and minds since birth.

Spirituality is a way to explore ourselves, reach enlightenment, and eventually, help others reach enlightenment and thus create a beautiful and compassionate community of souls.

It's all about peace and balance and a belief in magic and miracles.

The biggest misconception is that we have to follow certain rules to be truly spiritual. Or that we need a guide, mentor, or coach. *You already have what need inside yourself.* Some people search aimlessly, going from coach to coach, guru to guru, trying to find the meaning of life and their purpose. All it takes is some soul-searching. There are no rules. You don't have to eat certain things or believe in past lives. The common denominator is that you believe in something larger than yourself that is full of love. There is no fear or hate. There is no fear of God because *God is love.* A vengeful god, a god to be feared—that isn't love. That's what some have been taught. That's what has created the chaos and hatred in the world.

SURVIVAL OF THE FITTEST

Life is packed with lessons. All of life is itself a powerful single lesson. We are here to learn one simple and yet sometimes overly complicated concept—*to love and be loved*. Beyond romantic love, it's the unconditional love of everyone, despite their weaknesses and perceived faults. Most importantly, it is finding and embracing our imperfections and loving ourselves unconditionally, regardless of the observed ugliness, darkness, and weakness in our hearts. The smaller lessons, the ones you learn as you live your life, are personal. We are all unique individuals. We arrive in this world with genetic predispositions, born into distinct families and situations. Sometimes we are born into challenging circumstances. Poverty, trauma, abuse. Even those who are born into situations of kindness and unconditional love experience negative relationships and situations. It is all part of life.

We are thus shaped by our genetics and our experiences. Intense negative situations create patterns and behaviors that we carry with us throughout our lives. These eventually can become so ingrained in our mental and emotional being that we often act in self-preservation. Some adapt by becoming cynical, untrusting, and overly defensive, protecting themselves from pain. *I must survive at all costs.* That is, of course, emotional Darwinism at its most extreme. Survival of the fittest. If you survive the traumas and difficulties of life, you are a survivor. You defied the odds and made it through to become a successful, balanced adult. On the other hand, if you collapse, and your life falls apart, you are considered a failure, weak. Others judge you and you apply those judgments to yourself. You were unable to withstand the pain of the past and you failed.

What separates the survivor from the failure? Tenacity? Courage? Luck? A huge part of success is the capacity to have a positive outlook on life. With a positive outlook, you firmly believe that you can heal and in fact, work hard on yourself to heal. A positive outlook means that if you look at your experiences, good and bad, and perceive them as a step toward growth, life becomes more than just a series of positive and negative events. This is especially true of the "bad" things that happen. People often look at the negative experiences and think of only the pain and struggle. The bad is so difficult to comprehend, we swallow our sorrows, bury our pain, forget it exists. We often want to forget the experience. Alternatively, we may wallow in the pain of the experience, constantly reliving the events, letting the pain deeply affect our lives. We are often left with a fear of living fully. We live in safe-mode. Don't take any risks, no leaps of faith into the unknown.

So how does one person have a positive outlook and another a negative outlook if both had similar trauma in their childhood? Perhaps one person had more support than the other. Perhaps one person was genetically predisposed to the choice to heal. Or perhaps it was their chosen path, fate, destiny to come into the world and face certain challenges. It may have even been just one event that changed everything for the person who decided to heal themselves. One of those life-changing events that finally makes us wonder, *What the hell am I doing living this miserable existence?*

The pain and devastating emotions we feel at the end of a romantic relationship can be just as traumatizing as any difficult childhood. The pain can linger a long time, and healing can take many years. "They" tell you to deal with it. We are taught that we need to get past the pain and move on. But how can we heal if we just let it go and ignore the impact it had on our lives? The broken relationship did have an impact. You know how you felt. It did change you, your perceptions, the deep parts of yourself that you may not even realize absorbed the pain. Moving forward without healing, you may continue to repeat toxic patterns, or worse—you avoid allowing yourself to become vulnerable again and end up building walls that isolate you from deep human connection.

DISCONNECTION

In our hyperconnected world, we are extremely disconnected—from each other and ourselves. We can easily speak to anyone, anywhere in the world via text or phone. If we need something, it seems we can just pick up our phone and there we are—connected. We can sit on our mound of dirt, alone in our unkempt garden, push a few buttons, and spontaneously feel we aren't lonely anymore.

At least that's what we believe. Some people genuinely believe they are connected to others simply because of technology. Social media makes us feel loved. Or unloved, depending on who "likes" your posts or who ignores you. The definition of being "liked" on social media implies connection. People see you, they respond to you. Therefore, you're worthy.

We are all actors on a stage, "liking" because we feel we must. We can't ignore people—friends, family, or even acquaintances on social media. We feel guilty for not wishing someone happy birthday on Facebook. We feel pressured to "like" their posts. Why? Do we believe that they will then "like" us back? Why has it become so important, this social media façade? We tell ourselves so many lies to make ourselves feel better. Just because there are real people on the other end of the internet connection does not mean there is an actual emotional connection. Real, emotional connections with actual people are the only ones that matter. That's why we feel lost, lonely, and disconnected. There is no real connection in our technological world. The emotions we may feel, the euphoria of social media, aren't real. Most of what we experience is clutter, the mess that is the online world. We fill the hole in our garden with too much clutter, too much toxicity, and nothing can grow but weeds. When we eventually recognize this at a deeper level, when we discover we are still unhappy and dissatisfied even after everyone has liked our picture or our quote—this is the true moment of understanding that leads to awakening.

MIDNIGHT RANTINGS

Sleep. It would be wonderful to get more sleep. But I can't sleep these days. I wake up at three a.m., sometimes two a.m. Sometimes I don't believe I sleep at all. Thoughts fill my head. About myself, my future, and of course, the past. The utter failure of so many things. The anger. Things that fell apart, that didn't work out as I had envisioned. *I saw the future*. I saw images that showed a happy ending. Though they were foggy, I presumed those visions were about him. Most of all, I was angry with myself. For foolishly believing in something so far-fetched, so completely insane that I lost my way. I lost me. My identity. Sometimes I don't know who I am anymore. I never want to lose myself again.

Do I stay strong, remain solitary? Or take another leap? Losing myself terrifies me. But what terrifies me more is hardening my heart.

Sometimes I wake with ideas, brilliant concepts for stories, wanting to put them together, to create something beautiful. But lately, I am stuck. I try to write and I can only create one short paragraph at a time. The inspiration sputters. I've never had this problem. Usually, I write feverishly, filling many pages in a short time. Everything comes pouring out, insights, knowledge, revelations. My page is my soul, laid bare, honest, vulnerable.

Now, my late-night thoughts have been mostly about the past. I don't think I want to write about that anymore, so I don't even incorporate the past into my writing. I'm writing fiction. Making things up as I go along, weaving a bit of truth here and there, and trying to build a story by following the rules. It stifles me.

When I found myself sitting in my garden, still alone, after all my struggles to heal, I didn't know what to do. I didn't know what seeds to plant. I mean, I knew what I wanted, but I didn't know how to get where I needed to go. Which seeds would give me everything I wanted? I wanted to write, but not about the pain, the loss. I was done writing about love and loss. I wanted a love story. Not just for my character, but for myself. Nothing was happening. Nothing was growing. I watered and tended to my garden. Nothing but weeds.

I am the cultivator of my garden, I told myself over and over. *I am in control of my future, my destiny. I have released the past.* And I so badly wanted to move on, to nurture my magnificent garden.

If only it were that easy.

Looking back, I was simply trying to escape my pain, bury what I didn't want to see anymore. I wanted to complete the cycle and move forward. But something was still holding me back. There was still something I needed to do or to understand. I felt that in my soul. Something needed to happen to end the stagnant energy and propel me forward. I had no idea what to do or even how to go about seeking the knowledge I needed to tend to my garden.

My meditations were empty. I talked to myself, hoping to get answers. Aloud, I would ask myself the questions I needed answers to. I waited. Sometimes I would receive a message and it was simple—let go and move forward. *I know that!* I tried with all my being to let go, I tried not to think about it, reminisce, and I even decided that maybe it was easier to hate. I dated. I thought maybe that would help me forget. But every man I met, even if there seemed so much potential, seemed to walk away. Or I would walk away if I sensed any type of indecision. Was I cursed? I wondered why this was happening. I so badly wanted to move on and I foolishly thought another relationship was the way to do this. I didn't understand for a long time that I couldn't move forward until I resolved the conflict that was still within me. And that conflict was far deeper than I imagined.

So I continued futilely tending to my garden. Tired of pulling weeds and waiting, I let the weeds take over. I grew fearful. Afraid of failure, afraid of rejection, afraid of pain. That was not me. I had never been fearful. I was stuck. I wanted the Universe to swoop in and guide me, tell me what to do, tell me where to go. Do I leave the garden altogether? I wanted the path of least resistance, the path with no pain. I froze. Fear overtook me. I felt that whatever path I took would only lead to more pain. Any man I found would bring more pain. Every step I took would lead me back to the past in some way. I wanted love in my life. I wanted a man, a relationship, to be loved. I so badly wanted to be loved. I had so much love to give, I wanted to give my love away freely.

Forget the garden. I closed myself off, pushed through the weeds, and escaped.

I was in control. The Universe had abandoned me. I kept asking what was missing, *what do I need to do to move forward?* Waking in the middle of the night, I would plead for answers. And while a part of me felt empowered, brave, and confident, a larger part felt the complete opposite. I felt like a farce, a false healer. How could I heal others, how could I show them the way if I was completely lost and unable to heal myself? I was too broken. I lied. I lied to myself and lied to the world that I was strong, balanced, and pure. I kept up the façade for a long time.

I reached the point where I was tired of playing pretend. I took a break. I went off social media for a long time, I stopped writing, not wanting to share anything at all. It didn't feel real, and my heart wasn't in it anymore. I lost my way, I lost my love for what I wanted to do, and I lost the love I once felt for myself. I used to see all my past actions and events as lessons and learning, and I was grateful for everything, the good and the bad. But now, I loathed all the decisions I had ever made. I chastised myself for being so needy and believing in so many things that were lies. For proceeding through the red flags. I just wanted it to be done.

I felt that this moment was significantly pivotal. If I made the wrong choice, I would end up worse than before. It was perhaps *the* pivotal moment that would bring me to *the place*. Whatever the place was…would my next step determine the rest of my future? I would either soar or crash and burn. If you know me, you know that I have always been willing to follow any intuitive path without knowing where it led. That feeling was gone. I decided to use my logical mind, picking the path of least resistance and pain. The safe path.

I decided to take my life back. No more men. No more dating. If I ended up alone for the rest of my life, I decided that would be fine. Too much pain in love anyway. I planned my future. I decided to move. Far away, away from what I thought was an environment full of negative energy. In reality, I was simply running away from pain. And we know that you can't run away from your pain for very long. Eventually, it will catch up to you and you will have to face it. But I decided I would keep running. If it crept up again, I would move again.

NON-NEGOTIABLES

I once made a list of what I wanted in a man, in a relationship. A list of non-negotiables. The list ended up being fifty items long. I laughed at first. Could this person really exist? I didn't care. Those things all mattered to me. I even assigned the list to a character in my book. I made her crazy, obsessed, and a bit irrational. Funny thing though—as much as I laughed about my list and made fun of it when discussing it with others—deep down, I felt my list was realistic. I would hold out for him, for my man. In my mind, he existed, and it was only a matter of time before he showed up. He would be worthy of my love. Only him. Everyone else was insignificant, and I wouldn't waste my time.

Each time I met a man, I would mentally go through my list. If he lacked any of the items, each was a strike against him. Sometimes I would give it some time to see if maybe I was wrong. But I was always right. Some were easy. *My man must be emotionally available.* I could tell. So I walked away. The less obvious requirements took some time to discover. *Does he like to dance?* Nope. *Sorry, but we're done.* Yes, some of the items were very petty. But I wanted it all. I wanted the perfect man. Which I knew didn't exist. You would think after everything I had been through, especially understanding that perfection does not exist, that I would not see this as a crazy endeavor. I had accepted myself for who I was, with all my faults. *Had* is the keyword. At some point, I no longer accepted any of the things in myself that I saw as imperfections. I wanted to be perfect again. I wanted the old me to return. Those moments of lost faith, the moments when the non-negotiables seemed impossible and unrealistic.

The most incredible aspect of all of this was that someone did come into my life, someone who fulfilled all the qualifications on my list. I had thought it was a crazy, unrealistic list. I had dismissed it. *And then he appeared.* An unexpected miracle.

I had been tied to the past for so long, I didn't even know how stuck I was. Even when I escaped the garden, I didn't realize I still had dirt under my nails. It was almost invisible, small particles of dust. The old obsession had consumed every molecule in my body and soul, like a disease. Even as I cleaned the dirt away, bits and pieces would remain. I knew it would take time. I kept fighting, I kept clearing the dirt, waiting to return to the garden. I felt it was an endless task, but I kept on doing it. Sometimes I would wallow, uncloaking the pain and fears, doing away with hope and positive thinking. Other times, I would bathe in positivity and light, smiling toward the sun, knowing it would all be okay. Both of those were necessary. Sometimes we need to go to extremes as we heal. The key is to continue clearing the dirt and getting back into the weeds. Always focus on the clearing, even if you have to sit on a mound of dirt and not move for a long time.

THE GREAT DECEPTION

Looking back now, I can see where I went wrong and why. Always easy in retrospect. I felt abandoned. His rejection hit me deeply. Yes, I had always had a fear of rejection, like many of us. But this time the wound went all the way to my core. I didn't want it to end and didn't accept it. The pain was coming from somewhere. I thought I had felt love, I was confused. *How can someone love someone so deeply and still walk away?* I know it happens all the time. But I thought I had never loved someone as deeply as I loved him. That's what I thought at the time. It seemed impossible that something that felt right would end. Something was wrong. I looked at myself, and I knew it wasn't the real me. I was confident. But the pain pierced me because I thought he was the person I had been seeking all my life. He seemed so right. How could he go away?

Now I understand everything. But again, only in retrospect. I didn't accept the rejection. It was all about the rejection. I didn't want to be rejected. It wasn't about love at all. It triggered something in me that I didn't understand. Not at that moment, not when I was so immersed in fear and pain. I wish we could understand more in the moment. But then what would we learn?

I turned to the metaphysical for explanations as I was looking for answers to help me deal with the loss. I wanted reasons: *Why?* Why did something beautiful come into my life and then suddenly leave? I always got everything I wanted. I had worked hard, rising through several huge challenges, and in the end, I got what I wanted. This—this was not right. I believed I wanted this more than anything. Failure was not a part of my life. All those big things, I achieved through perseverance. That is what propelled me to continue to fight for the connection and a happily ever after with him. I didn't want to lose. I wanted my happily ever after. I reached a point where I was on my knees in pain. I prayed. I never prayed. I prayed for my pain to go away. That's how bad it was. At some point, I was suddenly filled with peace, which was followed immediately by the realization that I needed to heal myself, that I had deep wounds that had nothing to do with him.

Now I understand. He was a catalyst, a catalyst to force me to focus on my growth. I was stagnant, asleep, not wanting to feel or live fully. He made me aware of the fears that held me back. Through the pain of the rejection, I grew and moved toward living a full and beautiful life.

I was convinced he needed healing. I saw myself as whole, healed, and spiritually awakened. He was still sleeping. I wanted to wake him up. I was so wrong. It was me who needed healing. This connection wasn't love, not true love, but a mixed-up toxicity that made me believe it was love. It was a learning experience that brought me closer to the path to self-love.

BROKEN

Some survivors of trauma are viewed as strong and resilient. However, sometimes they have just built emotional barriers to protect themselves. *If I can survive that experience, I can survive anything,* they tell themselves. But that's the problem. Even those who see themselves as survivors may not have completely dealt with their pain and trauma. They may still be broken inside, even though they project a sense of balance. They rarely ask for help, believing that as survivors, they can solve all their problems on their own. Eventually, they become overburdened. The protection they have built begins to weigh them down. And they fall apart.

Some survivors, even those who haven't healed completely, decide to help others. A rape survivor becomes a therapist. They take on a different burden. This is a beautiful, giving gesture. But many unhealed healers are often in their own silent pain. Their healing is incomplete, and they immerse themselves in improving the lives of others, often at the expense of their own true happiness. Then there are those who keep choosing relationships with deeply broken people. We want to heal them, help them become whole because we are ourselves broken. Our empathy may eventually lead us to fall apart, broken and unsure of how or where to move forward in life when the other person moves on. We may keep moving forward. Never happy, but always helping others. There is nothing wrong with helping others—but you have to remember to heal yourself first. I think many, many people live this way.

The connections we build on our path through life have a direct impact on our ability to live in balance, as well as have an impact on others. We choose to either heal or remain broken. Healing, we move forward with positivity, exuding love and understanding. We create beautiful, positive connections with others. We love and are genuinely loved. Remaining broken, we create toxic connections. We are surrounded by pain and anger. The world becomes a dark place.

Deciding that you want to heal yourself, that you want to allow balance and joy back into your life, is the first step. You have to want it. That's why healing does come from within.

You must accept that you are broken. This is such a difficult admission in our world. We are taught to be strong and fight against the pain. Move forward, get past it. But the strength does not come from fighting the pain. It comes from accepting the pain. Once you accept that you are broken and you need healing, that makes you the strongest person in the world. While others will end up struggling the rest of their lives, pushing the pain away and ignoring the lessons that come from their experiences, you have already taken the first steps toward growth.

Be grateful that you are in this place. While there may be challenging moments still to come in the process, the hardest part, accepting that you are broken, is over.

LOOKING FOR LOVE

People spend so much time searching for love. Looking for love in all the wrong places, looking for love in too many faces...That about sums up human history. At least romantically. We don't even understand most of the time *why* we're searching for love. We just feel a need, an urge, a pull to have a companion. Some spend their entire lives trying to find their "perfect" someone. Some settle. Some find true love. Which one made the right choice? The seeker or the settler? The settler is at least at peace...right? But is the settler settling for a beige life? The seeker seeks a prismatic, rainbow life. Neither is wrong and neither is right. It all depends on your inner happiness. Whether you're a seeker or a settler, love may always be elusive until you find the love inside you. We can't fill the hole in our souls by demanding and desiring the love of others. Once we find the love within, then we can join ourselves romantically to others—love them and accept their love in return. There's a balance. You can choose beige or rainbow, but either way, it doesn't matter until you love yourself.

I think we humans believe we need to find the "perfect" mate to be happy. We may not even realize that we are searching for inner happiness when we search for a partner. The futility of it finally hits us one day and we begin to work on ourselves.

We continually search for romantic connections because our world creates isolated humans. "They" say: Be strong. Stand on your own. If you need help, you are weak. Especially now—all of the ways we are supposedly "more connected" have only caused further disconnection. Be popular. Have money. Be powerful. We feel inadequate. Then there are the amplified political and social divisions. A lack of empathy, respect, and understanding. More separation. In our hyperconnected world, we are consumed by loneliness.

Many search for love in romantic relationships because that's what society has told us to do. The happily ever after of movies and books. The desperate songs of love and loss. We want to see the main character get her man in the end. How often do we see movies where a woman ends up alone and happy? They exist, but I don't think they are as popular. And I get it. We want the happy ending we believe exists. We grow up thinking that's what we want.

That's what will finally make us happy. *We want our happily ever after!*

Life is about growth, the evolution of the soul toward love. It's not about finding the perfect love or having a perfect life. Those things are transient, just physical aspects of our reality. Those things won't matter in the end, as we journey into death. Besides, there is no such thing as perfection.

I choose a rainbow life. Perhaps it's riskier, not safe, unpredictable, and maybe even foolish. Beige is too normal. Too average. Safe and predictable. I'd rather have adventure and dive into the unknown. I've stopped seeking and trying to be "perfection." I just am. And I live and enjoy what comes my way. I believe there's more growth in the unknown. I do respect and understand those who want a beige life. I don't judge. It's comfortable. There is a lot to be said for security. But what if you go beyond the boundaries of your comfort? This is where the most growth happens. Eventually, you find freedom from pain, are surrounded by love, and reach the ultimate goal—surrender.

FREEDOM FROM FEAR

F ear is our greatest friend—as well as our biggest enemy. We fear so as to protect—it's instinctive. We fear to evade danger. Ironic, isn't it? I realized as I delved into my character in *The Misadventures of an Imperfect Woman* that some of the things I desired, I also simultaneously feared. Such a strange realization! I desired love, and yet, I also feared being fully vulnerable. I desired to be alone, yet I was terrified at the thought of being alone for the rest of my life. It didn't make sense to me until I understood that those opposites needed to come into balance for me to heal and move forward. Once I understood my fears and recognized their evolution, I realized what I was searching for was not the love of others or companionship, it was the love of self and acceptance of peaceful solitude. My solitude was anything but peaceful at times, with my heart and mind battling back and forth—so I desperately sought that peace that seemed unattainable.

I didn't want to fear. Yet I did. I did not want pain. But there it was. Eventually, I looked the pain and fear straight in the eye and said, *I'll take it, I accept it.* I embraced the fear and the pain, *the fear of the pain*, accepted them as a part of me, caressed them, and learned to love them.

That was the essence of self-love for me. Loving those things that had seemed so unlovable.

YOUR FEAR IS DEEPER

What is fear? Fears are a normal part of being human. We all have fears. The problem is when our fears prevent us from fully living life and finding joy in the present moment. Our fears are really about the future, what *could* happen, something that is out of our control. The fears overwhelm even our positive energy and we freeze. Past experiences trigger us throughout our lives, making us react irrationally. We fear the pain that follows abandonment, rejection, trauma, and abuse. These fears continue to haunt us in the future. We take fewer positive, necessary risks.

And sometimes, we take dangerous risks, never finding a balance, either living recklessly or not living at all.

The fear of pain may prevent us from allowing ourselves to be vulnerable because we fear a devastating outcome. We end up in disconnected and toxic relationships. We choose people who are just as broken as we are, people with similar fears. Both afraid of vulnerability. We increase our chances of becoming entangled in shallow, empty relationships, without emotional depth and significant meaning. We prevent ourselves from experiencing what it means to truly love and be loved. The real tragedy is when we wake up and realize we have wasted so much time. Our lives feel empty. Perhaps this will be your wake-up call—finally dare to face your fears and heal. Or perhaps you will move on to yet another shallow relationship. The choice is completely, and always, *yours*.

The fear of failure in relationships can significantly impact our decisions about future love. We may not directly fear pain—we fear failure in connections because that's all we've known. We avoid any sort of intimacy because we don't want to fail again. We're lonely and isolated, shutting ourselves off from any sort of deep connection. Even a shallow connection is avoided because you believe it will fail. Why try, if nothing has ever worked out for you? You walk away from everyone, because it makes you feel like you are in control—ending the relationship before it has a chance to fail protects you from any possible pain. Or so you think.

Nothing is ever lost. When you get your wake-up call, a second chance to find love, be courageous and face your fears. Refuse to continue the same cycle of pain and frustration.

LONELINESS

For some, the fear of being alone impacts their decisions and their way of living. We fear we will end up alone at the end of our lives, without a love to accompany us toward the end of our journey our earth. Especially if you are older, single, seeking the perfect counterpart to share your life with, that second chance at love. Time is ticking. Online dating is a mess. Meeting people in real life seems impossible. *How do we even do that?* Social events? Bars? People prefer the quickness, efficiency, and anonymity of swiping. Most people in the dating world are often as broken as we are, which makes achieving successful, loving relationships very complicated. A loss is a loss, whether by divorce or death, and we need to heal our grief before we can have a relationship with someone new.

We lose hope. And we worry. That worry compounds our negativity, and our positive energy is compromised. That positive flow of energy is essential to having joy in life, and the belief that all hope is lost keeps us stuck in negativity, making it even more unlikely that we will ever find what we're looking for—positive abundance in love. We may continue to endlessly date, moving from match to match, meeting people who we aren't interested in, forcing ourselves to seek "the one." Fearing a future of loneliness, we try to fill the empty void.

Sometimes our loneliness becomes a permanent state in the present moment, even when we are not alone. Even when we are surrounded by friends and loved ones, in the company of others, we can still feel lonely. An empty feeling, not being able to connect at a deeper level with those in our lives. Some of the time, this isn't really about the people in our lives. Yes, sometimes we are surrounded by negative, toxic people and we need to step away from them. But at times, our loneliness is like a hole, a deep feeling that something is missing—like a part of *us* is missing. We hopelessly try to fill that hole in our souls with material desires, addictions, and other toxic sustenance. The reality is the hole is never filled by anything in the physical. It remains until we heal and fill it with self-love.

The emptiness, the hole, exists not because we are missing something outside of ourselves, but because we don't love ourselves.

It's very simple. Self-love will fill that hole, that pain, the fear, and loneliness. Nobody else can fill that hole. Nothing else. You have everything you need already inside you to find your joy and fill your heart and soul with balance and love. Self-love is the only love that can fill the void. It's a difficult process, but very attainable. With work and honest self-evaluation, looking at why we don't love ourselves, we heal our emotional injuries, and eventually accept ourselves for what we are—beautiful, spiritual souls full of love and light.

This is spiritual therapy. While conventional therapy is often necessary, it does not comfort the spiritual self. Some of our wounds are beyond the physical. Some people need both, some thrive with just spiritual therapy. There is no standard therapeutic method. I am convinced, however, that spiritual therapy is a necessary component of emotional soul healing. While conventional therapy deals with emotions, as well as cognitive behavior, it does not deal with the deeper parts of our wounding, the kind of pain that can be described as existential chaos, deep loneliness, and the fear of living. The wounds that can only be healed through a mindful, deep investigation into our spiritual selves. Do you have to be a spiritual person to achieve balance? Maybe. I believe it helps to have some kind of faith in something larger than your physical self, be that the Universe, Source, God, or faith in your own higher self. You reach profound deep levels in yourself and create a system of self-support. When you understand that the energetic vibrations in our world, in everyone surrounding you, and most importantly in you, make a difference, you learn to raise your vibration. That's what spirituality is about—looking within, having faith in yourself and the world surrounding you, then raising your vibration to such a positive level that your fears are diminished, if not completely eradicated. And if the fears ever surface again, you easily recognize them, understand how to deal with them, and kick them out the door.

CLEARING THE WEEDS

*Fear of emotional pain is the root of every fear
and anxiety we experience in our mad existence.
The roots run deep and are difficult to clear.*

FIXING THE FEAR

How do we fix ourselves? Through the discovery of our fears. It sounds complicated, but it's not. One of the hardest parts of delving deep and identifying our fears is acceptance. Once we discover the fears that keep us frozen, unable to tend to our gardens, we begin to learn why.

You may already know your fears. Deep down, you probably do. If not, you need a way to access them. You may need to dig in your garden and bring them up to the surface. Uncover them through mediation and writing—there are many tools at your disposal, and we each have methods of introspection that lead us to those buried seeds that can't germinate. *Why would I want to uncover my fears and bring things to the surface that are buried "safely" away?* Do you want to live fully, and enjoy a life of love and meaning? There's your answer.

I fought my fears every step of the way my entire adult life. Fear of abandonment, fear of being alone in old age. Fear of rejection. These are all common fears, yet I thought I was alone feeling this way. I ignored the fact that others were also fearful. I was in my dark world of self-pity and victimhood. *Ah! The blindness that keeps us from seeing the truth.*

We are all fearful.

IT'S ALL YOUR FAULT!

When we're in pain or recovering from something that we think happened "to" us, it's easy to blame the other person. We are innocent, always. We can't see both sides of a situation when we are bound by heavy, painful emotions. Wrapped in something that may feel like trauma. We need to blame someone else, because we surely aren't to blame!

We fail to acknowledge our own part in the situation. Our actions and words, an irrational argument, unkind words, contributed to the end of something. Most of the time, both people involved are at fault. Is someone more at fault? If we try to assign a large part of the blame to one person, we miss an opportunity for growth. The only thing that matters is that both people made mistakes. Both people said things they shouldn't have. Both people acted in unimaginable ways. And if both are to blame, does it really matter who was more at fault? Can you really quantify that? It's like saying, *I love you 25% more than you love me*. It's childish and irrelevant. For an evolved soul, guilt does not matter. What matters is empathy and forgiveness.

When we feel so much anger and pain and blame someone else, we become bound to our pain. Anger and hate. Sadness and regret. We carry it forward, almost unwilling to move on. We get a rush telling our story, *our* side of the story, the "correct" side. *This is what they did to me, listen, and I'll tell you a woeful tale.* This isn't productive. We don't move on, we don't move forward, we are perpetually stuck in the wheel of pain and blame. It's a cycle, stuck on repeat. We carry it forward, entering into each new relationship as a martyr. Again, we find more pain. Again, unhealed from the past, we place the blame. That's why the saying, *We are the cause of our own suffering* is pretty accurate.

What if instead, we delve into healing? We forgive the other and ourselves? We accept the role we played in the situation?

No, it's not easy, and don't let anyone tell you that you just need to "let go" and "move on." It takes work—recognizing your pain and fears, acceptance, and then release and healing. You've got to start somewhere, and you won't know until you begin.

THE ONLY THING WE HAVE TO FEAR IS...

O urselves.

Fear of pain controls everything. Most people live lives driven by fear. We make safe choices. Choose secure lovers by choosing those that likely won't hurt us too deeply. Our feelings are muted. We love them enough, but we don't love them deeply. Instead of deep love, we feel mediocre satisfaction. Perhaps we fear being alone. We are anxious without a boyfriend, partner, lover. Perhaps it's the fear of being rejected. Rejection is painful, as is loneliness. But both of those fears are entangled. They are one: The fear of being alone. We wonder if our loneliness is augmented by the disconnection if the world. While the loneliness is in part a result of our disconnected world, we have to remember that the outside world if out of our control. What we need to understand is that our loneliness stems from our inability to love and accept ourselves, the gaping hole in our soul. We are disconnected from ourselves. It's much easier to connect with others when we love and accept ourselves. We fill our holes, and then we can fill our lives.

Sometimes we find love and we run in the other direction. Do we fear commitment? We would rather be alone than bare our souls, weaknesses, and shadow side to others.

Fear of pain controls everything we do. How we live is driven by fear of pain, and our thoughts and actions drive us to avoid pain. The fear of emotional pain is the big answer to every single fear we have. We are afraid of pain, which translates into many aspects of our lives. We fear being alone because sometimes it's painful to be still, to feel our pain, and move through the process of healing. We fear being rejected—there is pain in rejection. We fear vulnerability (afraid to share our real selves). We fear the pain of rejection (we aren't loveable). We fear taking a leap of faith to try something new. We fear the pain of failure. Fear of emotional pain is the root of every fear and anxiety we experience in our mad existence. The roots run deep and are difficult to clear. We fear. The fear of pain drives us to make safe choices, avoid conflict, and even protect ourselves to such an extreme extent that we lose the joy of living. We live like robots, always walking the safe and well-traveled road.

We rarely take risks that could lead to a more fulfilling and joyful life. We become accustomed to the weeds. We believe we can live amongst them in harmony.

Until the day when we can no longer move.

SHADOW WORK

Many of us go through life living in fear without knowing exactly why. We avoid certain types of situations and relationships even when others show us and tell us how much they love us. We build walls around ourselves, only letting small bits of emotion in or out. Sometimes we also do the opposite and enmesh ourselves entirely with someone, becoming co-dependent and creating a relationship not bound by love, but by need. Until we have done deep inner work, we don't recognize the extent or the type of fear that holds us back from forming positive connections.

One of the best processes to help you identify your fears and their triggers can be done right where you are, all on your own, without spending a single penny on self-development programs: Start a journal.

If you don't already journal, this is one of the best methods of connecting to your inner self. You can write daily or every other day. You can set a schedule or just write when you feel like it. I don't believe you should put pressure on yourself. Make it fun, interesting, and joyful. Some people prefer evenings. I find it's a soothing way to unwind from the day. Sometimes I just free flow, other times, I ask myself questions from lists I create. They can be deep, all-encompassing questions, such as, what am I afraid of? Or less intense questions—what attracts me to certain people? You can examine your life and choices and discover your feelings in each moment. Small things—move or stay put. Bigger things—love or fear. There is no right or wrong when you journal.

The point is to just start. Once you begin writing, I guarantee things will flow easier.

If you aren't a writer by nature, meditation is a beneficial way to relax and connect to your soul. Even if you are a creative person, meditation and daily mindfulness will get you centered and aligned so that you can relax. Let the answers, the wisdom, the words, flow. The words are already within you. You just have to access them and help them find a way out.

There are many options to start meditating if you don't have any experience. You don't have to take a class or find a mantra. You can do it by yourself or through guided meditation. YouTube is a great source for guided meditations. If you search, you will find many. You can also simply listen to any music that brings you peace. The key is to find something that helps you relax and clear your mind.

Don't be hard on yourself. The first time I meditated, I lasted about five very short minutes. My head was cluttered with thoughts—where's my shopping list and what was I making for dinner? Did I call about the stove? Why is that car parked across the street? After a few moments of just sitting there, bored, I stopped. I didn't think I could do it. And if you knew my crazy mind as well as I did, you would have agreed. But I went back the next day and tried again. And again the next day. Each day, I lasted a little longer. Each time I was less bored and distracted. It took me a while to reach the peaceful balance I was looking for. Many tries and many hours later, I was finally able to relax enough to eventually fall deeply into a state of nirvana. Now it comes easy. Yes, nirvana exists. Bliss exists. Without bliss, I would be in chaos.

JUST ME AND MY SHADOW

This is where things get deep and sometimes a little dark. But not scary. You need to do inner work, working on the dark, shadow side of yourself. Looking at your fears head on, shining a light into dark corners, bringing them into the light. Grasping those weeds and pulling them out from their deep roots, so they can't return. Accept your fears and then move on to understanding their evolution. Why do you feel the way you do and how have those fears prevented you from living your life fully and authentically?

Reflect on that. Write about it. Reflective journaling is much more than simply keeping a daily journal. Your journal serves as the vessel for everything that you want and need to release—emotions, thoughts, intuitive insights, crazy dreams. The key is that you write and then let things sit for a while. If you give things time to settle, when you go back and read everything, you will see new insights buried amongst your words. It's like reading between the lines. Looking at what you wrote and understanding that those words are coming from a deeper side of yourself. Don't judge your words as you write. Just write freely and honestly. Every thought or emotion is valid. Even if you think it sounds a bit wacky, write it down.

Conventional therapy can also help you delve into the shadow. We can all use someone objective to talk to in this crazy, chaotic world. Conventional therapy can help you to get past difficult memories or issues. Past trauma or abuse affects our relationships in ways we cannot completely see as we are living in challenging moments. Those core traumas at times can only be successfully dealt with in a conventional therapy setting. They are complex, and the underlying feelings need to be worked differently than spiritual therapy.

Mindful practices—meditation, introspection, writing—promote growth and healing. Meditation is key to developing a deeper connection to yourself. Those moments of stillness, where you stop the incessant inner dialogue, bring you to a place of peace, where you can just simply be in the moment. That peaceful state allows you to connect to your intuition, which will eventually help you make choices that are not based on fear. You may also receive messages or even have visions. You can have sudden thoughts that help you realize the reasons behind your fears. Whether you consider these as magical or divine isn't important—just accept them and label them in a way that feels comfortable to you. Journal all of this, no matter how small or irrational.

CREATION

F ear can be a spark for creation or a catalyst for destruction. We can take our fears, understand them, write about them, maybe create a story, or have an adventure that forces us to face our fears and transform our lives into a vision of positivity. Or we can take that same fear and let it destroy our lives. Never taking leaps of faith, having toxic relationships, never realizing our potential, and living a life shrouded by negative energy.

It's dangerous when we twist our fears into darkness. We don't go on adventures because we fear all the possible things that could go wrong. When someone offers us their hand in love, we push it away because we are just too fearful of the pain that may come. The fears build upon each other until finally, our lives are full of meaningless physical possessions or people that starve our souls. Our gardens are unrecognizable. We see what it means to live a life of desperation and insignificance.

If instead, we realize and accept our fears, we can create a new existence. We begin to look at the world differently. What was once dark becomes light. We may take that trip that we've been too fearful to take. We may take someone's hand and follow them in love. We may write about our fears and publish a book. We see what it means to live a life of joy and meaning.

THE ROSE

Every rose has its thorns—the more beautiful the rose, the more painful the thorns. Those words followed me and became embedded in my mind, my heart, and my dreams. A message from a wise, mystical healer. The problem was that I misunderstood the meaning. I lived in illusion simply because I believed those words meant something entirely different. At that time, I thought, because of my insane obsession that the rose signified a man I thought I loved. And even though there had been (and would be more) pain, it was somehow worth it because the rose was so beautiful. He was the rose.

I had plucked it, despite the thorns. The pain traveled through my body and into my soul. I was desperately sad, poisoned by darkness. I dropped the rose. It was too much. Too much pain. How could something so beautiful hurt so much?

Why me?

I gave up on roses. They were rare anyway and I had given up hope of ever finding one.

Then, unexpectedly, many years later, as I finally found a peaceful path through life, there was a rose right in front of me, perfectly positioned and freshly picked. Laid in my path as if someone had purposefully left it there for me. I wondered if it was meant for someone else.

Why me?

I wanted to pick it up, but I was torn. My impulsive side kept telling me to go for it, and yet, a small, very quiet voice somewhere in my head told me to stop and take a minute.

Coward. I'm supposed to pick it up.

It was the most beautiful rose I had ever seen. The fiery red petals were a deep flushed hue, passionate, the deepest scarlet red. It was tempting me, drawing me near, begging to be chosen. Yet, I was fearful. What if the thorns pierced me again? What if the pain was too much? Again.

I knew roses were rare, especially those that unexpectedly appeared out of nowhere. I resolutely chose not to be afraid. I edged closer, gingerly brushing the silky petals.

As I prepared to pluck the rose, I noted the stem was guarded with numerous thorns. I attempted to approach it from various angles, trying to avoid the thorns. Then I realized I would be pricked by those thorns no matter what I did. At first reticent, but eventually, with clear intention, I pushed my fear of pain aside, reached down, and carefully grasped the rose by its stem.

I examined the rose, looking closer at the folds of skin, the wrapped edges protecting the heart underneath. Suddenly the rose bloomed fully. The scent was intoxicating, and I fell into a deep state of bliss. Now I understood the beauty of the rose and regretted not picking it up sooner.

We all encounter rare red roses in our lives. Because of past experiences, we sometimes ignore them. We understand that beauty can also bring us pain. We fear the rose, but at the same time, we desire the exquisiteness of the experience. The intoxicating bliss. The more beautiful an experience, the more beautiful the path we travel, the higher the risk we will experience deeper pain. Loving someone deeply sometimes comes with being hurt just as deeply. That's what I used to think, before the rose. Now, I understand that deep love is worth the risk.

Would you rather wander off the beaten path and experience the bliss of the rose, knowing the pain that could come? Or just travel past the rose, always keeping your eyes on the future, the benign and narrow path? The safe path? We don't know what will come next, but we must have the courage to accept the pain that may accompany the joy. Overcoming the fear of simply picking up the rose, we experience life in full bloom.

INTUITION

Intuition is officially defined as "the power or faculty of attaining to direct knowledge or cognition without evident rational thought and inference." It may not be rational, in a conventional sense, because most people rely on what they can tangibly see or logically prove. As we know, it's a gut feeling, a feeling of correctness, a strong sense of knowing. Once you inhabit the stillness of meditation, you will start to build a deeper connection to your intuition. You learn to trust yourself and begin to recognize when you are acting out of fear. I firmly believe that balanced intuition is the key to making heart-centered decisions that will ultimately bring you to a peaceful place. You learn to live in the moment, without overthinking your decisions.

If you base your decisions solely on logic, you don't take necessary risks. Most of the risks we should take, those leaps of faith into the unknown, are *not* based on logic. If the whole world made decisions based on logic, where would the inventions come from, the new ideas and thoughts, the creative expressions of the soul, all those leaps of faith that have brought so much good to the world? You sense intuitively that a path is worth pursuing, even if your logical mind thinks it cannot work.

It may surprise you, but a lot of logical thinking is fear-based. We believe that when we think "logically," we are removing ourselves from our emotions. In some ways, we do this as self-preservation. *I love him, but he is too "complex," therefore I want nothing to do with him because complexity is not worth it.* Too much work and too much of a challenge. We are fearful of the pain of rejection, so we just walk away, believing we have made a logical decision. Everyone is complex. Everyone has issues. Yes, sometimes they are too much, and we shouldn't be in a relationship with that person. However, if we used our intuition to help us make choices/decisions along with some logic, we might find that there is more to this person than meets the eye and they might be worth taking a leap of faith. Picking up the tempting rose of love.

What does it mean to be intuitive? Some people call it the third eye, a sixth sense, a gut feeling, something you just "feel" and "know." A knowing. That's how I describe it. Knowing something to be true, even without clear and precise evidence or information.

I don't believe it's metaphysical or unique to certain people. Everyone can use their intuition. Most people do, without even knowing they are following their instincts. It feels right, and they do it.

Intuition is not full of emotion. It's a clear sense of something being right or wrong. Some think that a deep, sudden fear of doing something is a premonition, an intuitive feeling that you should avoid something. Intuition is balanced. More often than not, the fear, that irrational enemy, is not your intuition. It's just fear. It takes a bit of time to discern the difference between fear and intuition. It's difficult. Although I consider myself highly intuitive, I still have moments where I need to pause and look deeply inside myself to discern whether it's my intuition speaking to me or just plain fear.

Breathe. Close your eyes and feel where the fear is coming from. Feel the words of the heart and listen to the words of the mind. Sometimes they are in opposition, one saying GO, the other saying STOP. *Why why why?* Why go, why stop? The rational mind, the mind of overthinking will tell you because it makes sense, it's rational. *Listen to me,* says the mind. *I am concrete. I am solid. I am science and always real and right.* Logic does make sense. But is it always right?

The most important thing to remember as you work through this and finally can take a risk in love is that there may be pain. It is unavoidable in life. However, you will be armed with the knowledge and understanding that you can survive the pain. It won't hit you as deeply once you deal with the issues that prompt your deepest fears. Once you become balanced and open, even if you suffer pain, you will never feel it as deeply as you once did before you understood the control the fear had over you.

DARKNESS

Why are we so afraid of the dark? The shadow, the unknown. As kids, we fear those dark corners and for some, as we grow into adults, those dark corners continue to hold their power over us.

I used to be afraid of the dark. I couldn't stand total darkness, being unable to see anything at all. I always left a little light on somewhere in my house, just in case I needed to see my way through the dark in the middle of the night. It makes sense, right? You don't want to stumble and fall.

Fear of the dark is a fear of the unknown, what we cannot see, what we are afraid to see.

Stories since the beginning of storytelling, stories of things in the night, that slither from dark corners, are passed down to create fear in each generation. The stories of protection and self-preservation. It makes sense. Who knows what lurks in the dark? Humans need to protect themselves.

That is the physical darkness.

We just presume we can't see in the dark.

This speaks to the darkness involved in healing. Shadow work, sometimes called a "Dark Night of the Soul." Diving deep into your fears and pain, looking at those things through a spiritual lens. An honest lens, a necessary lens.

I'm sorry to tell you that you can't always be rainbows and unicorns. Spiritual development is not all about love and light. Don't believe that. You must go through the darkness before you can come out into the light.

I used to be only rainbows and unicorns. What I thought was a "perfect" blend of lovely light. I ignored the darkness. Told it to go away. It stayed, lurking in the corner as if waiting to envelope me.

I had someone tell me once not to talk about anything negative. Life is beautiful. And yes, I agree, life is beautiful. But you can't ignore the darkness. You will have to face it. One way or another.

It's not ominous. It's not hopeless or overly painful. Everyone makes it sound like it's the worst thing you can experience, going through a dark night of the soul. It's challenging, but the things we experience in the physical world are much more painful and harder to deal with. When you collaborate with yourself, with the Universe, you are collaborating on a much higher plane. You need to remind yourself you are protected.

When I finally confronted the darkness, I said, "*Okay, tell me what you know.*"

ACCEPTANCE

Acceptance of our fears can be the most difficult part of the process. I've already told you that many times. It's only to remind you that you shouldn't expect instant results and you will need to put in the work. *Accept your fears*. It sounds easy in theory, but when we look at these "negative" aspects of ourselves we very often want to deny them because they make us feel weak or imperfect. We rationalize that being fearful is a sign of weakness. Society constantly tells us to be strong, and that being fearful is an act of cowardice. *Just fight it, be strong, don't be a wimp.* This goes for both men and women. We are discouraged from asking for help.

Quitting is not an option. We are judged for not competing, for not pushing ourselves as hard as we "should." We are considered weak.

Sometimes taking a break from the chaos of living is needed. The reality is that it takes a lot more courage to face your fears, accept them, and resolve them in a personal way than to just ignore them. When someone tells you to just stop being afraid, they are telling you to ignore the fear, repress it and it will go away. It's unlikely that will happen, especially those very deep fears we may not be aware of. *Yet.* We jump right into new relationships, even when we are fearful of being rejected and hurt. We sense the fear and end up subconsciously sabotaging the connection because of our fear. And we don't even realize what we've done.

We want to prevent the pain, so we may end up rejecting the other person for no rational reason except for small things we pick up on, things we think mean that person isn't interested in us and is ready to reject us. We walk away, give up, and tell ourselves that they were about to reject us anyway. We confirm the truth of our fear again and again by walking away over and over or sabotaging our relationships in other ways. We deceive ourselves into believing that love is nothing but pain and rejection. We reinforce this time and again. Sometimes, we go in and out of relationships our entire lives, not giving them a chance to flourish, and not willing to put in the time and effort to make things work. We give up on love. We create our own fabricated reality and just settle for something safe but false.

Why are we afraid to accept our fears? Fear of imperfection, of weakness. There could be a myriad of other reasons. Take some time to write in your journal about *why* you are afraid of acknowledging the fear. Are you afraid of being weak? Of judgment? Of putting in effort to fix yourself and your situation?

THE UNATTAINABLE PERFECTION OF BEING

It takes courage to admit your fears. Especially if you are normally very hard on yourself and strive for the unattainable perfection of being. Fears are not weaknesses. They are a part of you, formed from your experiences in life. Good and bad events made you who you are today. If you are happy where you are today, remember the road you traveled. If you aren't completely happy, remember the road you traveled and accept the significance of the events of your life. Remember what carried you forward made you the unique being that you are, the one and only, the *you* that you are at this precise moment in time.

As we move forward, our minds create and learn self-preservation, protecting us from repeating the pain we have experienced in the past. Safely cocooning us from danger. Those fears may be buried or forgotten. It takes courage to unearth the fears and courage to acknowledge them. But just how do you find the strength and courage to accept the fears? Look within—it's there. Think about everything "bad" that has happened to you. *You are a stronger person because of those trials.* Think about the pain you have endured and the obstacles you have overcome. That is your strength. And that gives you courage.

Use affirmations. *I am strong. I am balanced. I am brave. I am at peace.* Meditate. *I am strong. I am balanced. I am brave. I am at peace.* Write! Connect to the courage within. Journaling is a key component of healing. Try writing over and over *I am brave* and say these words aloud daily. You will eventually find your courage. You create positivity in your mind and heart. Write it on your mirror, so you can see it every day and let it remind you what you are working on. I write words or quotes on my mirror: *I can do this. Love. Courage. I am loved.*

Remember—if you don't work on the fear, you will remain in the same stagnant energy. If you want to change, be a warrior, be strong, and accept the fears as integral parts of you that need a little love and healing. Everyone is fearful. Every single person on the planet has fears. It's how you deal with the fears and how you heal that makes all the difference. Those who ignore their fears will forever be stuck in negativity. Those who conquer their fears will move forward in life in a positive light.

LIFE IS A LESSON

What is the purpose of life? What is the meaning behind the everyday existence we lead? Why is it such a struggle? We have all asked ourselves these questions. It is deeply personal to each person. Some may find joy in creating, some find joy in relationships, family and friends, and loved ones. Behind all of these joyful pursuits lies the real purpose. *The purpose of life is love.* And the method of sharing and giving love is whatever gives you true joy and peace. If you are out of balance and your joy is limited, it's very difficult to give and accept love. Many will eventually strive for acceptance in the material world, attaining what they believe is power and wealth. Binding themselves to relationships based on security instead of love. We let the material define our meaning. We let others control our happiness. *We are out of balance.*

We are here to learn the meaning of love. The true, unconditional love of the self and others. The acceptance of unconditional love. Whatever that learning means to you. Sometimes hard lessons, sometimes small understandings. From the day we are born until the day we pass into the light, we are here to learn. There is no end to learning. If you see life in this way, and you look at your experiences as lessons, good and bad, it makes life less stressful. You don't have bad or good luck, and you do have some control over your life. If you look at the negative not as another terrible thing that happened, but as an opportunity for growth, you ease the negative feelings associated with the experience. You reclaim your power. It's not simple or easy, but it is possible.

Of course, most of the learning happens after the challenging events. Sometimes as we move through challenges, it's very difficult to see outside of the experience we are immersed in. Very difficult to be objective. What will help is to write about the experience. Then go back and examine what you wrote. Understand, evolve, and grow. If you go through something difficult and never think about what you learned or examine your feelings and actions, you are just going through life in a daze, half asleep to the beauty of life, disconnected from yourself. Your mind plays tricks on you and your emotions follow along. Clear your mind by opening your heart and growing.

The key is to understand, learn, and move forward, seeing clearly, but not dwelling on mistakes and pain. If we don't learn, we will likely keep repeating those same endless patterns, those same toxic behaviors, and ultimately recreating the same types of relationships. If we were scarred by emotionally unavailable people, we will continue to choose those same relationships, until we finally learn how our fears affect our choices. We keep cycling, pointlessly trying to fix our past by repeating the same scenarios over and over. We want to get it right, fix the past, and force someone to love us. We will continue to seek, either consciously or subconsciously, the same types of people and try to make it work. We are desperate for resolution, thinking that others can heal us. We forget that only we can heal ourselves. Not another person. Not a lover. *We are responsible for our own healing. We have the power to heal.*

We need to stop the vicious circle. If we notice these types of behaviors in ourselves, or if we constantly blame others, we need to understand—we chose those toxic people. There are plenty of balanced people out there to choose from. We just keep choosing the wrong ones. They are as broken as we are, and two broken people together likely don't stand a chance of making any relationship work. All you do is create a toxic, co-dependent relationship, full of unhappiness, which ultimately affects your self-worth, lowers your self-esteem, and most importantly, causes you to lose hope and give up.

Perhaps you think you can change those people. That's another pattern we get caught up in. Those people, those lovers that we blame for our stuckness and who we think we can change, also need to do inner work, and it is not up to us to fix them or heal them. Only they can heal themselves. *Only you can heal yourself.* And you have to want it. If there is no desire to change, then there is no desire to heal. Many go through life in pain and suffering until they finally realize this. They need to work on themselves. And sadly, some never change and end up living a lonely and miserable existence.

Learn your lesson. If you keep going through these patterns without learning, you will continue to meet the same people and have the same types of toxic relationships. Examine your relationships and your casual dating. Is there a pattern? Do you seem to be attracted to emotionally unavailable partners? You are not "unlucky." You keep choosing these people, so you haven't learned the lessons. Once you examine the relationships, once you find a pattern, then you can tie it back to your fear and pain. If you don't trust people and see them as shady, you will choose to date untrustworthy people. They lie, they are sneaky. You have an "a-ha" moment, when you realize, that many of the people you have dated are this way. Take that knowledge and tie it to your past pain. Did someone who should have been trustworthy betray that trust? If yes, then you know that the fear of trust stems from your childhood. Perhaps it was reinforced later in life by a partner. Or simply, a single failed relationship based on lies or a deception led you to believe that people are not to be trusted. Regardless, armed with this knowledge, you can begin working on your healing. You begin to unravel the reasons behind your relationship failures. As you work through, you understand that you kept choosing these people because you were trying to heal yourself by putting yourself in the same situation, hoping for a resolution of your fear and pain.

Once you work on those issues, either in conventional therapy, spiritual therapy, or both, you learn that there are people you can trust. There are people who are emotionally available. Your fear is the result of the pain you suffered in the past. Once you learn the lesson, you can move on to a more stable, balanced, and nurturing relationship.

To help you understand, you can write down as many details as possible about each "failed" relationship. What exactly happened? How did you feel? Did you see any red flags early on? Usually, the red flags are there, but we ignore them. You learn to identify those red flags much earlier and more easily after you finally see what you chose to ignore.

THE MOST IMPORTANT LOVE OF ALL

We love others and we want to be loved in return. Sometimes we mistakenly believe that if others don't love us, we are not worthy. Our quest is to find someone who loves us, hoping to find happiness in the arms of another. *All we want is to be loved.* Throughout history, our society has placed a huge emphasis on romantic love and how important it is to be loved by someone. As if it is the end-all. Don't get me wrong, being loved is extremely important. However, the most important love, the one that gives us confidence and the ability to understand our value, is self-love.

Until we love ourselves, it is very difficult for us to accept love from others. Once you love yourself and find your joy, others will openly share their love with you. The most important concept of self-love is that *you are the only person that can make you happy*. Not someone else. Not someone else's love. Once you love yourself, unconditionally, you will no longer have that feeling of lack, as if something is missing. The great big hole in your soul that you believe can only be filled by others or through material things, can only be filled by you.

Finding that love of self is challenging. We are our own worst critics. We find fault in many things we do; we judge ourselves harshly when we make mistakes. Because of our past experiences, we believe we are less than what we are. If we've continuously been treated badly, we begin to believe that we are not worthy of love—from others or ourselves. The whole key to self-love is accepting who you are, the good and bad, and loving yourself unconditionally regardless.

Know your value, your worth, and all that you have to offer. You are a beautiful soul, a unique being. Others may never see your worth unless you can see it yourself. Nobody is perfect. We are perfectly imperfect. If we were all perfect, and there was no pain or negativity, how could we appreciate the beautiful, happy moments? You need the yin and yang, the balance of the spirit. It all ties back to lessons and why we are here. To learn to love. If you look at humans as spiritual beings, put upon the earth to learn more about love, to evolve, and to enlighten, then you can see...

We are all connected.

CONNECTIONS

We are all connected at an energetic level. We are composed of particles of energy, based on quantum physics, and these connections are as mysterious as they are magnificent. We may have started from a single energetic particle, and the particle infinitely multiplied, creating the universe, planets, and life. Stardust. This energetic connection keeps us all bound together, passing energy back and forth, good and bad. The key is to keep the positive energy flowing, moving from person to person, like sharing your light on a dark night, each person touched by another, until we prevent the passing of negative energy.

That is why sometimes we have encounters with people to whom we feel a deep connection, a bond that surpasses the physical. Energetically, we remember the connection at a deep level. Sometimes those connections are so powerful, especially in romantic encounters, that we can't quite explain these feelings. We feel as if we have already met this person, we already know them at a deeper level. We are happy and comfortable, but at the same time confused about how something can feel so close to us, so much a part of us. Why do we meet these people? Is there a reason, a purpose for the connection? We wonder.

The people we meet in our lives, the deep connections that are sometimes inexplicable, serve a purpose, or multiple purposes. Perhaps these people come into our lives to help us learn and grow—to teach us lessons about ourselves and the Universe. We may recognize in others, consciously or not, certain aspects of ourselves that need to be healed. Looking into the eyes of another, we often see our reflection. And what is reflected back is not always pleasant. A mirroring of our faults and imperfections.

Some say that these are soulmates or even twin flames. Some believe that these people shared past lives with us, and we recognize them because of that past connection. Maybe we have unfinished business from our past lives and we needed to meet again to resolve whatever karma still remains. Or maybe, it's just pure, real love, a soul connection that brings us joy and fulfillment.

Whatever the reason, the most important aspect to understand is that we are all connected and everyone we meet, every encounter we have, happens for a reason. Someone who holds the door for us at the grocery store, someone who teaches us something important—everyone serves a purpose on our journey through life. Appreciate everyone—without them, you would not be who you are now.

DEEPER CONNECTIONS

Those blissful, deep connections that seem to be instantaneous can be very confusing. Blissful because of the joy the connection brings to our hearts, our very soul. The feeling of love we experience may be beyond anything we have ever encountered. We feel a sense of home—safety and security; we belong together. We *need* to be together. It feels like a nostalgic pull to the past. We feel a deep sense of unconditional love.

Although many of these powerful connections are romantic—many seem to long for their soulmate and that special connection—some connections are meant to be friendships. Many jump into a romantic relationship with these deep soul connections and soon find themselves in a very complex and complicated emotional situation where everything seems out of control. The pursuit of romance, sex, and commitment creates more confusion, since many of us perceive romantic connections as the most important ones in our lives. And while they are important, friendships are just as important.

Much can be learned from a powerful connection. These people have entered our lives to teach us. Because we feel a sense of safety and security, we are likely to become more open and allow ourselves to be vulnerable. We reveal aspects of ourselves that we may have never revealed before, sharing our fears and exposing our shadow side. We grow from this, learning more about ourselves and how we connect to others and eventually moving into an awakened state as we become enlightened souls.

Complications arise when a romantic relationship is not meant to be romantic. One or both people might not be ready for a deep romantic connection. But there are lessons to be learned. While it can be blissful, usually the learning that needs to take place is painful. Perhaps one or both of the partners becomes fearful. This creates conflict and one or both will run away from the other because of the intensity of the emotions that have been dredged up. This causes pain for both. However, if we remember that pain and conflict often lead to growth, and we work through our own fears, we can learn so much about ourselves and evolve into a balanced state. When we suffer a loss and go through pain, we come out on the other side, wiser, more intuitive, and more loving. We may fear the pain, but it comes nonetheless, propelling us into a dark night of the soul, where we finally explore our shadow side.

Usually, it is our very fear of pain that causes more pain. We fear love, we fear being open, we fear rejection and abandonment. Yet these deep soul connections bring all of these fears right out into the open, right in our faces. We are forced to learn and grow, we are forced to heal our fears. We delve deep and find greater insight into not only ourselves but also the other person. *We understand*. If we are abandoned, we are thrown into emotional chaos. But we must bounce back. We must heal. *We know this*. For the most part. We learn that we need a positive way to heal, not just repress our pain and move on, but face the fear of pain by allowing the pain to come in. We must experience the regret and sorrow of a broken heart to heal our souls. We can't hide it away, bury it, or even worse, we cannot create a self-deceptive illusion where we believe everything will work out if only...we put in the work, we change the other person, we figure out a way to control the situation...you get the idea. None of these are healthy ways to deal with the pain. They are just another escape.

THE IMPOSSIBLE WEEDS

Some people never heal. That's why our world can appear to be such a chaotic and hateful place. People just forge ahead, not understanding the lessons or the growth that is needed for them to move forward with positivity and love. We become angry, bitter, and resentful. Cold and lonely, seeing the world as pain and only pain. We may become very good at repressing and building walls to protect ourselves. We shut people out, hide our emotions, and deny our vulnerability. Yes, we succeed at keeping the pain at bay. However, sadly, we also prevent the joy. We become stunted. Stuck.

Unable to live a beautiful life of deep connections with others, beyond romantic relationships.

There is love in everyone. Even those whom we may perceive as "evil." They are souls who have not healed from childhood wounds, haven't yet learned the lessons they were meant to learn in this lifetime. Some people say you choose your life before you are born—the challenges, the growth—so that you can become a more enlightened soul. Whether or not you agree with that, the fact does remain that the hate that seeps into the world is because of a lack of healing and the fear of pain. It is difficult to have faith in humanity and yourself if you believe that people are inherently evil or hateful. If humanity is intrinsically evil, what do you then believe? That things cannot change? There are aspects of the world that have always been and will be evil? If you believe that, you cannot believe in change and the power of redemption. Without faith in humanity, you will lack faith in yourself to heal and grow and ultimately live a joyful life.

You don't have to accept the hate and simply walk away from initiating change. Far from it. You can heal yourself, then venture into the world to make a difference in the lives of others. One soul touching another, bringing love and light to the lost and dark. Others find hope in your actions and words, and it propels them to move toward their journey of discovery and healing. Each person touched by another, creating a web of connectedness and a community of enlightened individuals, and ultimately a more enlightened and loving society.

LEARNING FROM THE PAST

What have you learned from looking at your past romantic relationships? Think about lessons you have learned from both successful and failed relationships. Don't dwell on the heartbreak—the pain will engulf you if you reside too long in the emotions. Instead, think about what you learned—the positive aspects, the lessons. Then you can reflect on the negative aspects. You learned that you fear being vulnerable, but did you also learn not to trust people? Create that list. The good and the bad, the dark and the light.

Look at your list. Do your positives outweigh the negatives? You are stronger and braver. You know what you want and what you don't want. You know what makes you happy. This is the path to follow. Your list may contain many lessons. Or just a few. What is incredible is to see the words and understand what matters to you. You have gained insightful knowledge of what you want—and don't want. Think of how far you have come. You are still alive. You have survived the worst—all those events and emotions are in the past, and now you can examine them with an open mind and heart. And you learned so much in the process. You are grateful. From the pain, from the weeds, you grew into a mighty, strong oak, able to withstand anything.

You've learned what you want and what you will not stand for in a relationship. And once you find your value and worth, others will see this in you and treat you how you deserve to be treated.

THE NON-NEGOTIABLES

Create a list. Everything that you want in a partner. Those non-negotiables, those things you don't want to compromise. Be honest. Be real. Without judgment.

As I mentioned, when I first did this exercise, I wrote down over fifty non-negotiables. Way too many, according to other people. I didn't think so at the time though. So I kept my list and referred to it periodically. As I met men and crossed them off my list of possibilities, I soon realized that there was probably no man alive who could embody all the characteristics of my list. But it was an important exercise, because then I came to realize there were some things on the list that perhaps didn't matter to me as much as I thought. However, I refused to give up my non-negotiables, even though at that point I was celebrating my imperfections, while at the same time, searching for a "perfect" man. Eventually, I whittled down my list. Now it's only forty-nine requirements. Seriously, I did narrow it down to fifteen non-negotiables. It was more realistic. And more open-minded. You open yourself to more possibilities and unexpected, beautiful surprises.

Then he arrived. The man who somehow satisfied every single item on my original crazy list. That's when I understood. The list mattered. All the non-negotiables were embodied in a man who came into my life when I least expected. However, it wasn't about the list. It was about the release of the list. I let go and there he was. The best part—he had even more to offer than was on my original list. The openness and release brought even more beautiful, unexpected love than I had imagined.

Simply make a list of some of the non-negotiables that define what you are looking for in a relationship. Must your ideal person be emotionally available and honest? Or is it more important that he/she be compassionate? What matters to you? Just put down every single thing that matters to you, even if it seems unreasonable or unrealistic.

Examine your list. Is it long or short? At first, I called it the "Impossible List," because finding this man seemed impossible. And then I edited my list, trying to be rational and reasonable. But I didn't need to edit my list! What I wrote was important because it obviously created something magical. The Universe gives us unexpected gifts sometimes, once we release the expectation. Once I found my joy and the pleasure of solitude, no longer craving the love that seemed so needy, that's when the gift arrived.

The exercise of paring down your list is helpful. You begin to clearly see your true wants and needs. This is important to understand so that when you meet someone new and something important is missing, you will know right away. It may be an intuitive feeling or just simply something visible and out in the open. You may choose not to pursue the relationship any further if there is something significant this person cannot give you or the relationship.

In this way, you learn to break the pattern of choosing the same types of people. The endless, toxic cycle of the lesson that is never learned, as you continue stuck in unsuccessful and painful relationships. You may not understand why the people you are with are not emotionally open. You blame it on them and maybe even feel you are cursed or that all potential partners are closed and broken. And what do you learn by blaming them? You have simply blamed them for something they cannot necessarily control. You chose them, remember that. You may have even chosen them for their lack of emotional availability. What was the lesson you needed to learn? To stop choosing emotionally unavailable partners. You learn that you are in control, that you have the power to choose who you want in your life, and that nobody enters your life without your permission. So we need to stop blaming others for problems that are our own doing.

Again, *we are the cause of our suffering.*

When you do the work and realize *why* you keep choosing the same toxic people, then you begin to understand. Then you start to learn and evolve. When you meet people, you are more in tune with your intuition and can sense right away if something is amiss. You will no longer waste your time on toxic relationships. *You know who you are and what you want.*

I LOVE ME

Self-love is truly the most important love of all. It's not just a saying. Loving yourself, you can give love and accept love freely. If you don't love yourself, you will never be truly happy, living a fulfilling life of joy and purpose—it will be elusive. Without the love of self, you will encounter many challenges in relationships, particularly romantic relationships. Occasionally, someone may come along who is understanding and will help you bolster your self-esteem, and perhaps even help you heal from feelings of inadequacy and low self-worth. But those people are rare. It takes a soul filled with so much love and a depth of understanding. Most people are not as enlightened as that. If you don't love yourself, how can you feel worthy of someone else's love? You will never feel good enough. You may unconsciously sabotage your relationships, pick toxic partners, or fall into co-dependent relationships. Always seeking the love and approval of others, instead of finding your worth and value within.

Once you love yourself, truly accept and love yourself and all of your imperfections, you will never allow others to treat you badly. *You will not allow it because you know your value and your worth.* You know you are worth loving. By loving yourself and allowing only positive treatment, self-love enables you to receive and give unconditional love, creating a balanced relationship with equal give and take in many aspects.

So how do you love yourself? When you look in the mirror, can you look yourself in the eye and tell yourself, "I love you just the way you are?" Try it. It's difficult and uncomfortable for many. If it is difficult or uncomfortable, think about why. Society has taught us that loving ourselves is selfish. We must always give our love to others and love is often measured by what we give—and what we give is not always love. Some try to buy love with expensive gifts and extravagant material expressions. Do you understand the beauty of someone picking you a bouquet of wildflowers instead of buying you a bouquet of perfect roses?

Some people are also self-centered and only think about themselves and even wildflowers are too much to give. Those are people who do not love themselves. Their outward selfishness and focus on self, their narcissistic behavior, is simply a symptom of low self-worth. They are simply trying to bolster themselves and fill the void, the hole in their soul. They lack empathy for others and desire to take control of people and situations, perhaps manipulating others with guilt and shame.

Loving yourself is not selfish. Saying we love ourselves is not narcissistic nor does it make us self-involved. It is a true expression of the love of everything and everyone—if we are all connected, by loving yourself, you send your beautiful loving energy out into the world for others and shine a bright light on the whole universe. Perhaps even loving yourself can help change the entire energetic vibration of the Universe into one of love. Other people around you, connected to you, pick up on this. They decide they also want to make a positive change; they want to be like you—they want to make a difference.

THE DESTROYER OF SELF-LOVE

There are many complex reasons, besides the societal ones, that cause people to feel a lack of self-love. Childhood trauma and abuse create emotionally and spiritually broken humans. They feel unworthy and unloved. *Why would anyone love me* is the negative self-talk ingrained in the soul of the unloved. *If I'm treated badly, I must be unworthy. If I am rejected, I am unlovable.* The patterns keep repeating as the person continues to immerse themselves in toxic relationships. They believe that they don't deserve happiness or love. They don't even realize what they've done.

Their subconscious has taken over. They ask themselves over and over, *why do the wrong people keep coming into my life?*

Repeating patterns. The souls who don't love themselves are continuously repeating the same pattern to fill the hole in their souls. The lack of love, lack of self-love, the emptiness that keeps them stuck. The only solution they know is to seek love outside themselves. Fill themselves with the acceptance of others so they can feel worthy.

The definition of trauma is personal and can take very ordinary forms. While the feelings of loss from heartbreak may not seem traumatic to some, it may be for others. The level of the trauma is not measured by the event, but by how the event affects each unique individual. One person's seemingly trivial pain is another's trauma. And what may seem like a horrific trauma from the outside somehow doesn't break a person. We are all unique and feel things differently. You don't need constant emotional or physical abuse to feel the pain that creates the feelings surrounding trauma. You can develop PTSD from one single event. Everyone fears pain and when the pain overwhelms and changes how you approach life, and you begin to fear taking chances, you avoid certain things, you repeat toxic patterns. You have been affected enough by an event that you will eventually require healing of your spiritual wounds.

GARDEN OF SURRENDER

*That's how you move through healing. Knowing and accepting.
Then eventually surrender.*

TOUCHING THE SHADOW

Spiritual work is about the healing of the soul. This involves working with your shadow side. Our shadow is the very deep part of us that we keep hidden from others—and often ourselves. The parts we don't want to face or expose to the world. The dark emotions we feel, the fears we don't want others to know. Shadow work can be very complex. The fears have been hidden in darkness for so long—we have to figure out how to draw them out, while at the same keeping our balance as we work through the intense emotions.

I often think of Peter Pan, who lost his shadow. It kept running away from him. Or did he subconsciously keep himself from facing it directly, pushing it away? At one point, he fights his shadow, hoping for it to return perhaps? Or maybe to take control? Perhaps he is fearful of his shadow side—the fear of growing up, learning, evolving. Change.

Connecting to your shadow is not difficult and it does not have to be a battle, as long as you are willing to come to terms with what you find. You should delve in with a positive, non-judgmental attitude. You may need some support—a friend, a spiritual therapist, a mentor—or you can work on your own. Join a tribe of like-minded people (there are many free spiritual groups online, as well as in person). There you will find support and understanding. It takes a Universe. Getting support from others who are spiritually aligned with you is sometimes essential.

Through meditation and reflective journaling, you can connect to your soul and write down your ideas, thoughts, emotions. You review what you wrote and reflect to get a fresh perspective. This is how you connect with your shadow.

Write and home in on what you fear about yourself. Some people call these faults or weaknesses, but they aren't—they are simply a part of you that needs love and understanding. You are a unique individual, and your "faults" are merely imperfections. And imperfections are good. They are what make you *you*. Nobody is perfect. Thankfully. If you try too hard to be perfect, you will never be happy. I spent my entire life trying to be the perfect everything—mother, wife, daughter, friend—until I realized how unhappy I was. I finally looked within and went on a quest for self-discovery. I know who I am now. And I love myself, imperfections and all.

And finally, acceptance.

Discover your shadow. Make lists. Look at the imperfections. Don't be afraid. Start small. If you feel unloved, understand that many of us feel this way at various points in our lives. Nobody wants to admit this to others. We believe it makes us seem weak or unhinged. Being vulnerable and sharing things that we think others will not understand is the key to growth. We release the fear of the judgment of others. *Accept it.* It is who you are. Accepting the shadow, then you begin the work of discovering why these aspects have affected your actions and behaviors. Do you run away from relationships and unconditional love? Do you self-sabotage?

DON'T FEAR IT

Look to your past. Always look to your past experiences to explain your fears and the resulting shadow imperfections. The key point to remember when you are examining your past is that they are memories, and the past can no longer harm you. The fear may still exist, but you are protected. The event is over, done, and no more harm can come to you as you face it. Always keep in mind why you're doing the work—the end goal. You don't want to continue to be stuck and live your entire life in pain. You want to rise up and out of the shadows, take your imperfections, and love them unconditionally. Regardless of where your fear and pain arose from, regardless of who or what caused the pain that resulted in the fear, your shadow trait, tell your imperfect, beautiful self, *It's okay. I am here to make sure I am healed, so I can move forward and live a joyful, meaningful life.*

Get out of your head. Don't let your negative self-talk take over as you delve into the dark. Firmly tell yourself: *I will discover my shadow trait, I will accept it for what it is, and I will heal the wounds that caused it to arise. I will work on it by analyzing and understanding the reasons why it evolved. And I will heal the fears that prevent me from moving forward.* There is no point in holding on to broken relationships, clinging to false hope because you fear that a connection like this may not happen again—that he is your one and only.

Many people come into our lives for various reasons, romantic and platonic, and you should not fear that by letting go, you may end up old and lonely. Especially if you are older. I used to fear being alone. That I missed my one true chance for happiness in love. But I realized there can be many new beginnings and many other possibilities out there and the most important thing is loving yourself. That is what true love means. Be happy with who you are, love everything about yourself, and always, always stand in your power. This is when a life-long soulmate usually walks into our lives.

EMPOWERED AND STANDING IN YOUR TRUTH

Standing in your truth. Many don't realize the importance of speaking up for yourself. With or without fear. You need to have the confidence to say what you think and feel, without the worry of judgment or consequences. It doesn't mean that you should be spiteful or mean. What it does mean is that you speak from your heart, share your vulnerable emotions. Share your thoughts. Be kind and truthful. Become compassionately empowered. For some, all it takes is that one moment where you allow yourself to say what you think and feel. You find your voice and you find your power.

This is empowerment—you are self-empowered to gain knowledge and understanding of the self to find self-love and ultimately take control of your life and your future. Speaking up without worrying about judgment, you are confident.

Empowerment is not something anyone can give you or teach you. It's also not something anyone can take away from you. It's within you and a power only you can acquire and express. It's about healing and self-love. Once you love yourself, you realize your value and your worth and you don't allow yourself to be treated badly.

FORGIVENESS

I'm sorry. Sometimes we long to hear those words from someone who has hurt us. Sometimes those words will never come. We need to find a way to move forward.

Forgiveness is a huge component of healing. Not only forgiveness of others, but we also must forgive ourselves for the choices that brought us down a painful path. Forgiveness is difficult. We hold so much anger and even sometimes hatred toward others who have hurt us. We blame them for causing our pain. The reality is they have their own spiritual and emotional wounds that perhaps caused them to act a certain way or say hurtful things. You need to remember that forgiveness is for *YOU*, not for the other person. While releasing the burden of their guilt is important, that is their issue to deal with and not your responsibility. The important aspect is you need to release your anger and pain so you can let go of negative emotions and move forward.

Forgiveness has to come honestly. You can't simply say, "I forgive you" and be done with it. You have to mean it. It's not easy. Once you have an understanding of your fears and your pain, then you can forgive. You realize your pain was not caused by their actions; it was a result of your own reaction. It comes from you. Then you can forgive. You don't have to confront the person or send them a message. This isn't about that. This is for you. You can imagine the other person is present, and say, *Despite everything you did that hurt me, I forgive you*. Repeat it as often as you need to, until you feel the release of a huge burden. You are carrying negative energy—the anger, the pain, the fear—that pulls too much focus away from the positive and living your life in full. So, learn to accept and forgive.

We forget, though, that the most important person to forgive is ourselves. We often look back on the choices we made and feel disappointment and anger for our own "mistakes." There are no mistakes. Every choice we make leads us down a path. Sometimes there is pain, sometimes joy. We learn along the way and we grow. Sometimes we can't see the entire road ahead of us. We don't know the future. So we make choices based on our best intuitive knowledge, which can sometimes be clouded by fear. Regret is very often worse than the pain we suffered. It can consume us to the point that we are unable to move forward. Forgive yourself for your choices. You didn't know what would happen. And most importantly, those same choices formed you into who you are now. Who you are now is a beautiful soul who is willing to work on yourself and grow. *You are not a victim. You control your destiny.*

LET IT GO

J ust let it go. Let go of the past pain, the obsession, the desire, and the hope. Easy, right? Not really. People say this all the time and make it sound so simple, so easy. As if you can just tell yourself to let go and move forward and it's done. The past is in the past. Apparently, if you don't let go and move on quickly, it's your fault. You're weak. Something is wrong with you.

The reality is that it sometimes takes a lot of time and effort to let things go. People, situations, feelings, emotions—releasing the negative requires shadow work and examining the past. The past is gone and cannot be changed. *That you must accept.* However, you should go and explore your behaviors and emotions that landed you in the unkempt garden. You examine through writing and meditation and look at things with clarity of mind and openness of heart. Don't sugarcoat it. Shadow work will have you look at things about yourself you may not feel comfortable accepting. That's the hard part. Once you accept those things, you will find it much easier to release the pain from the past. You might not want to admit this, but you were and are responsible for many of the things that happen in your life. You create your reality with your thoughts and emotions. If your obsession is wrapped around rejection, then it is likely you will be rejected. You will fall into situations where someone will reject you. We create our reality, over and over, until we learn enough to move on.

You also need to want to release limiting beliefs and ideas. Often, we don't want to let go because of fear. All the usual fears—loneliness, last chance for love, rejection. We hold on tightly to that which we want because we fear the future and what we may not get. Holding on tightly, we feel that this love fills the hole that is in our soul. We think that empty feeling can be filled only by someone's love, their presence. But that's not true. We are only trying to fill an empty part of us with love from others—love that we should be giving ourselves. Finding our own happiness in our own adventures. Finding joy in small things. Gratitude. Once we move toward healing, we realize that the void is filled. A long process, but isn't it better to have the love surrounding you all the time, the self-acceptance, instead of waiting for someone else to fill the emptiness?

A LEAP INTO THE UNKNOWN

The future is unknown. The only truth we know about the future is that there will be death, one day. The rest is unpredictable. While I believe in many things, I don't believe anyone can predict the future. The psychics that tell you your true love will walk in the door any minute, begging for forgiveness and wanting you more than life itself, are merely looking at a possible future. The future changes with every action, breath, and thought that is taken in life. I go right instead of left, and my future is forever changed.

We have the power of free will. Even if you believe the Universe intervenes in certain situations to try to make something happen that is "destined," that does not mean it will happen in the way you expect. You may choose to walk away from someone, even after something mystical happens in your life that is guiding you toward someone. You don't have to follow the path that is being shown to you.

While we may be fated to meet certain people, and perhaps even mysteriously drawn toward them in synchronistic ways, we are the final masters of our destiny. We may move forward at full speed, or we may turn in another direction. We have the final say. That's why the future is unpredictable. And that's what's so scary. We want to know what's going to happen, so sometimes we become so obsessed that we seek out psychics and tarot readers, hoping that they will tell us what is to come. We want to know. *Is he coming back? When?*

Many believe psychics, tarot readers, palm readers, and others with divination skills can predict the future. They spend significant amounts of money on readings, hoping to find out what will happen in the future. However talented these readers are, whether they are gifted or not, does not matter. Nobody can predict the outcome of anything, only a *possible* outcome. The future is not set in stone, ever. Even if there is divine intervention, we have free will and the future can be changed at any moment. Many believe those psychics who claim their lover will return, money will magically come to them, and they will be live happily ever after. They believe and then do nothing. They wait. If it was foretold, it must happen.

So they sit. And wait. When that future doesn't come, they are disappointed, angry, and perhaps even feel deceived. They were, but they also deceived themselves, believing that someone could tell them what was to come later. Remember that. Nobody can predict the future.

I spent hours watching tarot readers on YouTube. I was fascinated by how they interpreted the cards. Some claim to feel the energy. While it is true that some can intuit the energy, how do we know who is intuitively sensing the energy or simply making things up? Very often, the readings are about love. Always a tale about someone who is brokenhearted, because someone has walked away from them. The souls in pain want to know when and if their lover will return. Sometimes people are caught in toxic relationships and patterns. Sometimes they are lonely, desperate for romantic love. Many more are in situations of unrequited love and claim they were abandoned by a twin flame and are awaiting the lovers' return. These souls live in misery—always waiting, always stuck. Many believe the words of the readers and the most popular ones are usually the ones that say your lover is returning to open his or her heart and apologize. It's an industry that takes advantage of those who are in pain, filling them with false hope and illusion. They know what sells. While it is beautiful to have hope, relying on the words of those who are there to make money is a tragic dependency on false hope.

There are many people out there who are in pain. Suffering, lonely, desperate.

I'm not disparaging tarot readers. Many don't just try to predict outcomes in love and instead focus on the spiritual development and growth of the individual. The evolution of the individual and how we can attain balance and joy, without the need for a partner, are far more instructive. If a reader says someone is coming in with a love offer, that will be true for some, but not all. Pick and choose your reading and you can believe anything.

As for twin flames, I believe they are not meant to be challenging relationships per se, where people wait years (yes, some people have been waiting years) for their "true" love and twin to return to them. Meanwhile, they may have done little self-improvement by always relying on the misleading advice of others, and they live a life of always looking toward the future without living in the present moment. Perhaps they may even have missed out on other amazing relationships. Perhaps their pain will linger for the rest of their lives because, in reality, they haven't healed. True love is there and waiting—sometimes everything has to come together at the right time. Spending your life waiting is not a productive way to exist.

People are desperate for answers. They want to know what is going to happen. They want to take leaps of faith, but they need to know their chances of success. So they become addicted and obsessed with trying to predict the future. Taking a leap of faith means doing something without knowing the outcome. Trying to verify an outcome defeats the purpose of taking a leap.

Those who walk away and are committed to leaving a relationship are more than likely to stay away, even with divine intervention. And that's a good thing. Would you want someone in your life who is so conflicted about you? If they suddenly returned, wouldn't you wonder why they are back? Are they healed? Healing takes time and the desire to heal. Most people who live in fear, so much fear that they walk away from love, do not want to face their fears and heal. And yes, it sometimes does happen that a huge life crisis—a tower moment—suddenly forces them to look at themselves and understand that their lives are a mess and that they are a mess. Maybe it's divine intervention that swoops in and causes a crisis, encouraging them to open their eyes. Or they create their crisis through their actions. But they need to want to heal.

As we move toward the future, we absolutely need to take risks. We don't know what's going to happen, even if people tell us that they can predict our future. Sometimes even our intuition, clouded by fear and deceptive thoughts, is wrong. If we make decisions based on fear, we are not using our intuition. You may not know all the facts to make a logical decision. That's why you need to trust your intuition. Crystal clear. No fears. No strong emotions. You leap, even with some fear of the unknown.

Just know that no matter what happens, you will be okay. If you feel pain, you will heal. The leap will likely take you somewhere amazing and beautiful. *Even with pain*. If you experience love, *it will be worth it*. You learn, you grow, and the experience becomes part of your journey.

READY FOR LOVE

How do you know when you are ready for a new love, ready to take the leap of faith into a beautiful union?

Do you jump in, especially if you experienced heartbreaking pain? You need to heal. Without healing and understanding, moving too quickly will likely result in disaster. You will just get caught in the same cycle again, especially if you don't understand the lessons you learned from the previous relationships. Perhaps you will continue fruitlessly searching for a deep connection with someone, seeking the old love in the new. You will be sorely disappointed. You cannot go in search of love. Believe me when I say that love finds you at the right time. It's something that happens. If you look at every new date as a potential soulmate, you will not find your soulmate. Love comes when you least expect it—as trite as that sounds, it's true.

You will never find your former lover in a new love. That soul was unique, and nobody could take his or her place. That connection was special because it was unique. Two unique souls, bound for a moment in time, in a union that cannot be repeated. You will meet someone new, with a distinctive kind of deep connection. You will feel love, you will feel a connection just as deep and just as amazing. Or you will find something even deeper and more amazing. You may realize that the old connection is nothing compared to the new one.

Once you have healed and are ready to love and be loved, then venture forth. Go slow if you want. You don't need to be intimate right away. Sexual intimacy is an exchange of energy and if you are not ready or the other person carries some negative energy, it will become infused in your energy. Then you're likely to get confused again. Get to know the person. Build a strong emotional connection. We all get caught up in the throes of passion, and it's tough sometimes to say no, especially when you feel that strong bond. All you want is to feel the other person physically.

Hold out and wait. The new relationship might end up being something you don't want, it might be wrong, it might be toxic. And while casual sex is not a problem for some, I think you have to be in a certain mind frame to do that. Yes, free love may sound spiritual, but perhaps it takes two very spiritually evolved and emotionally mature people to forge that bond. I know people do it all the time. I've been on Tinder. I've been propositioned on the first date. I know many people just want to hook up. If that's what you're looking for, I'm not judging. But I do believe life is meant to be about establishing deep, meaningful connections with people. Too much casual sex points to fear of vulnerability, fear of pain. People close themselves off emotionally. Plus, with every sexual encounter you have, that other person's energy becomes a part of you. And not just their energy, but the energy of every other sexual partner they've had. If you are an empath, you will soak it all up, and that can deeply challenge your emotional energy.

SOLO JOURNEY

She felt she was on a solo journey. She knew she had to be on her own right now. Being with someone, regardless of the seriousness, combines the energies of both. His energy would become a part of her, an entanglement. *I need to be in my own energy.* It was a growth period, a time to focus on herself. She should have done this a long time ago, but back then, she didn't understand what she was supposed to do. She finally found happiness on her own. And when he came along, she wasn't ready for the entanglement yet. She still had things to learn and more growth to experience. It's something all people need to do. She needed to keep moving in her independence to create a life that was balanced and, in many ways, pure.

There is depth to life that can only be found by walking a path alone. Sometimes it's lonely and sometimes you want companionship. *They* always say good things come when you least expect them. If the timing is off, it won't work. And the timing felt off to her. She tried to create her life each day. Each moment was a creation. She wasn't lonely. She cherished all of her experiences and lived in the moment.

She didn't understand logically why. She tried to explain it to him. It's a *knowing*. And intuitive. And she had to follow her intuition because she believed it would lead her to expansion and growth. Those times she had ignored her intuition, things became messy.

You're a friend. I don't even think I love you. You are not him. I know.

She continued writing, trying to gently explain to him they weren't meant to be together.

We connect with people randomly. Sometimes it's just for learning, but other times it's to collaborate to bring something beautiful into the world. Words, music, art. Those are the types of collaborations that are meant to happen. The physical relationships sometimes enhance the collaborations, and other times, they create things that aren't good for us—not because there is anything wrong with people, but simply because the energies don't mix in the right way. It's like alchemy. You can have the perfect ingredients and even the right combinations, but sometimes the mixture or ingredients need some time to simmer before they can blend into a perfect combination.

She spent so much time searching for love. We all do. Sometimes we don't even know that's what we're searching for. But that's what we all spend our lives doing. It will always be elusive because the love is inside us, we carry it within, and we can't fill the hole in our soul by desiring the love of others. Once we find the love within, then we can reach out to others, love them, and accept their love in return.

I'm still sorting through some of the lessons I learned and still have some things to unravel. I don't think I'm ready for love. Every day, I learn something new, and I cherish every experience and growth.

I'm happy.

And she knew *he* would come soon.

MANIFESTING

While I do believe in the power of positive thinking and feeling emotionally balanced, I'm not certain I believe that you can manifest absolutely anything into your life. General happiness, abundance—those are possible. Specific people, or wealth, power, and other very material things, are not part of our soul purpose. The whole concept of manifestation is defined too broadly. It should be about manifesting those things that are for your highest good or the highest good of humanity. Love of all people, a life purpose, peace. Cars, houses, money—those are material desires of the ego. Do you believe those things can make you truly happy? Is there only one person that can fill your soul? Are any of those things you're trying to manifest in your highest good?

I'm not skeptical. It's just that people believe those material things, including the love of others, will bring them happiness. The point of manifestation is about drawing positivity into your life. If you focus on the positive and are grateful for what you already have, your whole attitude changes. Your thoughts change and that affects your emotions. And your emotions are tied to your intuition, which carries you through life. If your emotions are off balance and you desire something for the wrong reasons, your intuition will be off. As you go about your daily life, feeling confident, happy, positive, and loved, you will attract more of the same. *If you exude love, you will attract love.* This is the higher purpose of living. We attract what is good and meant for us as spiritual beings—those things that bring us into balance and alignment with the Universe and our purpose.

We create our reality through our thoughts and actions. We create positive and negative emotions based on our thoughts and actions. Filling ourselves with positive energy, we open ourselves to many amazing possibilities surrounding us, waiting to be manifested.

Some claim to have used manifestation to achieve success in love and money, simply by making vision boards or writing down their desires and wishes. However, I think there is much more to it than that. By creating these visions and dreams and focusing on them and working hard to achieve them because of the confidence instilled by the positive energy, those manifestations became possible. It's not magic and it's not a secret. Sitting around waiting for things to happen while we manifest our little hearts out, doesn't work.

You may want a Ferrari or the love of your ex, but those things are desires of the ego, the physical, and not the needs and wants of a true soul enlightened by love. More often than not, those desires are simply our need to fill the hole in our soul with outside things, instead of striving to love ourselves and live a purposeful and meaningful life. Sure, a Ferrari may make you happy, temporarily. It's fast and fun, but when the fun wears out, you are still left with a hole in your soul. When you've made millions and don't know where to spend it anymore because nothing gives you pleasure, you are left with a hole in your soul. When you desire the love of someone who does not see your value and worth, and they arrive different from what you expected, you are left with a hole in your soul.

We are constantly searching for meaning in life. Desiring understanding and knowledge about our existence. There has to be more to life than we what see in the physical.

When you do finally unconditionally love yourself, you understand what it means to love another unconditionally, that's when you begin to attract love. The difference between this and the material—it's energetic. Our molecules and cells react to the positivity so that when we encounter other people, they feel our uniqueness, our special love. And they desire us. This is especially true if we attract someone with a high positive vibration like ours.

They will recognize our energy and want to get to know us better. You will recognize each other as beautiful souls.

Think about manifestation as a way to bring beauty, joy, and peace to your life. All you need is a positive attitude, immense gratitude, and patience.

A positive attitude stems from positive thoughts, which create positive emotions, and in turn, raise our vibration to attract positivity and love into our lives.

VIBRATION

Sometimes we meet people and are instantly attracted to their energy. We can't necessarily put it into words, but we sense something about them that excites us and pulls us towards them. That's because they are vibrating at a high frequency. High-vibrational people know they are worthy of love and happiness. They appear confident, even extremely charismatic. In many ways, like attracts like, so when your vibration is high, it is presumed that you will attract people who are positive and energetically similar.

The problem is when someone with a much lower energy frequency is drawn to you and vice versa. You might be drawn to someone because even in your high vibration, you can still have parts of you that are healing. You can still be attracted to someone with those same toxic qualities you are trying to separate yourself from. Perhaps they shower you with attention. You can't see past their actions to see their true nature. They are a little more broken than you, and those lower-vibration people simply crave your positive energy. They need something to give them a boost, help them with their healing. Most people do not understand this concept and that their vibrations are not a match. You may feel the pull to the other's energy and they sweep you off of your feet. You are drawn into yet another relationship where you give and give and all they do is take.

It's not even a conscious decision. You are both entangled in each other's energy. You want to fix them, and they acquiesce. If the higher-vibration person is not aware of how this energy works, they will fall into a very unequal relationship, where one person continues taking and gives nothing in return. The energy vampire can suck you dry at times, taking all of your energy until you feel tired, depressed, off balance, and ultimately, desperate to get out of the relationship, but still blaming yourself for the mess that you're in. You lose your confidence and your belief in your self-worth. You want them even more and give them even more because somehow, you blame yourself for everything.

This type of relationship will have little chance of success. Eventually, the higher-vibration person will grow tired of getting nothing in return and will pull back. The lower may get angry and arguments ensue. Or the lower will simply threaten to walk away.

The relationship becomes a co-dependent dance. The giver keeps giving in desperation, hoping to hold on to the taker, who has realized the hole in his soul is still there no matter how much the giver has given.

GRATITUDE

Why is gratitude important?

Being grateful goes beyond being thankful. While the two words are used interchangeably sometimes, they are different. Gratitude is a general appreciation of life—it's a feeling rather than an experience. Thankfulness is a response to a particular event or experience—feeling pleased or relieved. You can be grateful for your family, but thankful that your cousin showed up early to help you set the holiday table. You can be grateful for the community where you live, but you are thankful that your neighbor brings your garbage cans up from the curb on a rainy day.

Having a grateful attitude impacts your life and your emotional and mental balance in amazing, positive ways.

Gratitude is a mindset. It's a way of being, a way of living. Being thankful is a moment, an expression of thanks for a kind action or a turn of events that made everything more beautiful or just simply better. A stranger holding a door for you. A beautiful sunrise. A deep hug from a friend. I'm thankful for that sunrise, it filled me with gratitude for all sunrises, for this day.

Gratitude means being grateful for what you already have, despite all the negative things that may be happening in your life. Finding our own happiness in our own adventures. Finding the joy in small things.

Like attracts like—being grateful for what you have despite what you lack or the mess that is currently your life—will create even more things to be grateful for. Just like a positive attitude brings more positive energy into your life, if you notice everything around you that you are grateful for you will soon understand the full meaning of gratitude.

Amidst all of your confusion and healing, you can appreciate the beauty of nature. Appreciate all the sunrises and sunsets, the water, stormy days, and clear starlit nights. I take pictures of nature. Even though those images are in my head, seeing the pictures reminds me of the awesomeness of nature and that it will always be there—something to look forward to every day. Something to be grateful for. I love my long walks along the river, the time for quiet contemplation. It removes me from being in my head.

Be grateful for the food you eat—you have nourishment while many lack food. With gratitude, relish the flavors, the experience of cooking, the opportunity to create something delicious. Add spices and flavor and experiment with all kinds of unique recipes. Change the ingredients, making everything taste better. Beyond sustenance, food is an experience, an almost orgasmic bliss of sensations. Savor every moment of eating.

Traveling, experiencing new cultures, and learning the history of mystical places, I am in my element. The newness of each experience gives me peace, as well as a recognition that there is so much more to life than trying to find a perfect man.

Sometimes, even in those moments of pure joy, where I expected that I would cut loose those desires for a man, I felt a slight sadness. I wanted a companion to share those beautiful moments with, someone to be by my side, to fully connect with me and the experience. It wasn't about having someone there to make me feel better, it was about the shared moment. Looking at the beauty of those moments—I desired to share them with someone I loved. It was complicated. I didn't like that feeling. I felt ungrateful, and it seemed too much to ask—for a companion, for a lover, a partner. *I'm sorry for asking for more, Universe.* I fought it sometimes, telling myself that it wasn't normal. I should be happy and grateful; wanting something else to be added to my life was wrong because it somehow ruined my gratitude. *Be happy for what you have,* I would tell myself.

The words momentarily brought me back to gratitude. It took me a while to understand that it was fine to want a relationship. I stopped fighting with myself. I realized I was trying to prove that I was healed and to heal meant letting go of my desire for a man. It took a long time to accept that this was quite a normal feeling.

JUDGMENT

That was my problem, I was constantly judging my feelings and what was "right" and "wrong." I wanted to do everything right. It was part of my desire for perfection. Perhaps just to prove to myself and others that I was whole, and wholeness meant not wanting anything, forcing myself into gratefulness. But it's a human condition to want. It has to be accepted. There is no such thing as a "normal" feeling. Feelings just are.

We often judge our feelings as either good or bad. The important part is understanding why you want something so badly and knowing whether it will complement your life or simply fill a void.

The saying *you can have your cake and eat it too*, I changed to *I already have my cake, and a man is just the icing*. That's probably why I treated men with such contempt. Why couldn't I just mix him into the batter of the cake? Because there were so many failures in dating and relationships, I decided they would sour the flavor of the cake. This was my cake and I chose a safe recipe.

It was empowering in many ways to realize I didn't need them in my recipe. I was content on my own. You can't have true happiness until you find that joy alone. If you're always searching for a perfect man to make you happy, you will always fail. I eventually learned that I wanted to add them to my recipe. Not out of need, but desire. No more judgment—only acceptance of what I wanted and felt.

SOLITUDE

The joy in solitude is true. While there can be days of loneliness, once you learn to cherish your solitude, those days are rare. I spent many days on my own, mostly writing. Sometimes the loneliness would come when the character in my book needed to go through something difficult. I embodied her, her fiction became my life—and her life was pretty emotionally challenging. But I didn't stop writing, because it helped my character become more human and helped me accept many things about myself. We became entangled, and I sorted through the emotions of what it meant to be a single, older woman in an insane digital dating world.

All of us, men and women, are broken and healing. Everyone has had different challenges, and it takes compassion, understanding, and kindness to connect with another person in a meaningful way. I lacked in those in the past because I was self-centered. But that's the human way. We are about self first—it's all about *me* until we learn to let go of our ego. I knew with that new understanding, I would venture back into dating eventually.

My solitude became extremely necessary for me. I occasionally felt like one of those writers you hear about who lock themselves up for years in a cabin to finish their books. I was now one of them, even though I wasn't sure most of the time what the hell I was writing about. Being with others made me feel like I was being forced to share her story too soon—perhaps they could sense my story through osmosis or pick up on my emotions, and the story would be corrupted. It wasn't a memoir, it was all fiction, yet the story I was telling touched me at such a personal level, I became my character and didn't want to share it with anyone. At least not until her journey was complete. Until my journey was complete. *Our journey.*

SHOULD I OR SHOULDN'T I?

There is nothing wrong with desiring companionship, a lover, deep love, and a strong connection. Yet we fight against wanting those sometimes. Our world pushes us into wanting those happily-ever-after endings, while at the same time telling us we don't need each other. It's so complicated, a push and pull. There is nothing wrong with desiring companionship. It's normal to want someone to share things, to be a part of your life. It's also normal to live in solitude. We have to accept what we want and have the courage to move toward our desires, without worrying about others' thoughts and judgments of our chosen lifestyle. We can grow in solitude or companionship. We can thrive in so many ways, and it's not up to others to choose our path.

We create opposites within us. The "Shoulds and Shouldn'ts." I *shouldn't* feel a certain way, which is especially true. Feelings just are, and you cannot judge them as right or wrong.

1. *I feel broken.* Is the brokenness of people a detriment? No, the brokenness of people creates understanding and enables us to be compassionate.

2. *I feel incomplete.* I love myself, filling the void with positive words and actions. My incompleteness is a part of my healing. Life is healing and nothing is perhaps ever complete.

3. *I feel a lingering sadness for lost love.* I am grateful for experiencing that kind of love.

4. *I feel trapped.* I'm only trapped in my mind, I created the trap with my fears. It's okay to feel trapped because from that experience comes growth.

5. *I judge others too harshly.* I judge others too harshly because I judge myself too harshly.

6. *I am weak.* There is no such thing as weakness. Claiming and accepting your "weakness" is strength.

7. *I hate men/women.* Everyone shares the blame for every-

thing. Recognize your part in situations.

8. *I am impatient.* Be patient with others and yourself during healing.

9. *I'm not always grateful.* Try to take a moment and feel gratitude for little things every day. Journal!

10. *I cannot forgive.* Figure out a way to forgive others and yourself. Ask for forgiveness from others and yourself as part of daily meditation.

11. *I have no control.* This is a truth. The only thing you can control is yourself. All else is chaos and you need to learn to let it go.

12. *I don't have love.* Love is everywhere, feel it, exude it. Love for others, love for yourself, despite the faults you may perceive.

13. *I have no power.* You can't control others, but you can feel empowered by making choices for your highest good and not hurting others in the process.

14. *I'm in pain.* It's transitory, let it flow through you and it will pass. It's a good thing, it teaches and heals.

15. *I fear.* Fear comes from not dealing with the past, but dealing with the past sets us free. We all fear.

16. *I made mistakes.* The past can't be erased, but learn from it. Forgive and move on.

17. *I hate these feelings.* Feelings just are.

THE SYMPHONY

She felt and heard the musical notes, each with its specific emotional tone. In the cacophony, each individual note was recognized, as if it stood alone. Her eyes were closed, and although she could not read music nor understand how it was composed, she understood the meaning. She was serenaded by each sound, each note telling a different story. The low, slow notes quietly whispered the sleepy tones of her life, and the higher andante notes accented the moments of utter joy. The high notes pierced her, reminding her that those moments stood out for a reason. They were the ones to be remembered, those significant memories that changed the whole tune from a steady flowing rhythm, one that was almost too still, to one of significance. Who wrote the beautiful piece? Again, she closed her eyes and took it all in. She listened, and again and again those distinctive notes were felt as moments of joy. What were the composer's feelings as she wrote? Did the music evoke different emotions from each listener? She felt fear, love, passion, and a little anxiety. Each note was a change, and she realized that change scared her sometimes. At the same time, it was exhilarating, fresh, a moment that had to be experienced or all of life would be mediocre. She listened until tears came to her eyes from the sheer beauty of the composition.

In her mind or a dream, she saw a mirror. She reached out, touching the mirror with her fingertips. She felt a vibration. The passage of the music from the other side of her reflection seemed to influence everything. The room vibrated, and her body pulsed in an identical rhythm. It was heard and felt. With her eyes closed, she perceived vivid colors. Hues of green, orange, blue; a rainbow of sounds.

Then it suddenly stopped. She opened her eyes in disappointment. She wanted it to continue, she wanted it to remain part of her and her life. It added so much beauty. She looked into the mirror on the other side of the room, waiting. Nothing happened. The vibration was gone, the colors and sounds disappeared. *Please come back*, she said aloud. She wanted to be part of the music, letting it carry her through life. She wanted to step into her reflection and into another world. What she didn't realize was that music had already become part of her. Simply hearing the music, she had absorbed it into her soul. The composition would stay with her forever. Every note remembered. She became part of the other world.

WEB OF CONNECTION

Human connection is invaluable. We are all connected energetically. Living in emotional isolation stunts growth. These energetic connections, especially those with emotional depth, are what allow for our expansion as loving, spiritual souls. These deep connections go beyond the simple, everyday acquaintances. Although casual connections are also important in other ways, the deep friendships and romantic relationships where we connect at a deeply significant soul level are the ones that have the most impact. We are not afraid to be our authentic selves in these connections. We are comfortable. We feel at "home." Our comfort allows us vulnerability. This is important because, at the very basic level of our existence, we often feel alone. We have been socialized to see ourselves as apart and distinct from others. We focus on ourselves and our desires first and foremost. The "I" seems more important than the "WE." This has become a normal part of the human condition. Me. The I. The Ego. How we experience things is based on our singular, hyperfocused perception of reality. Everything that happens, happens *to* us.

If instead, we start to view ourselves as all intrinsically connected, our perception changes. Our beliefs, thought patterns, and behaviors change. We realize that everything we do affects everyone at an energetic level. If we are imbued with love, we exude love. If we are permeated with fear, we exude fear into the world. The fear creates a negative energy pattern that surrounds us and is then absorbed by others. People are pushed away. We disconnect. We turn more inward, finding ways to protect ourselves from the chaos that appears to exist outside ourselves. We dissolve direct, deep connections to other individuals. We isolate ourselves. We may still be extremely social and outgoing, going to events, parties, dating, and raising children. Normally active and participating fully in life. Inside, however, we feel alone. Unbalanced. Broken.

Connections we make in our lives, those that affect us at a soul level, those that help us find our place in the Universe, sometimes cannot be explained. They are meant to be that way. When we're deeply connected to people, we learn. There is a purpose that brings awareness. A deep connection, one we never want to end, strong love, sometimes not romantic in nature, is a soul-level connection. Those soul connections guide us toward our soul purpose. It's a mutual relationship where we teach each other and then move forward, either together in a lifelong romance or in a lifelong friendship. Be grateful and forgive. Take what you've learned and experience the growth. We are still being guided and we will be guided our entire lives—if only we pay attention.

    I'm still learning. I've been on this journey since awakening. *I'm still learning.* I keep learning and growing and that's part of life. We evolve. We will never reach perfection, but we will reach a higher state of being, so significant that we change our perception and way of living. Then we can pass our knowledge and love along to others in how we live. We live authentic lives, and others see this and strive to live the same way.

SPECIAL LIGHT

Everyone has a magical, special light inside of themselves. Every single person on the planet. Once you find it, you connect to your soul and learn what truly matters, what your higher purpose is. It may be a lifelong journey, in and out of darkness. Or a short moment in time. Once we love ourselves and find that light, then we can make a difference in the world. We are special. We are love.

BLISS

What is bliss, nirvana, serenity? I believe it's different for every person. For me, I feel a sense of joy and calm, and also an intense connection to everything, including the deep parts of myself that are usually not on display throughout the day. In these moments when we are in that deep connective state, we can access the thoughts and emotions that we hide away during our daily lives. In these moments, don't be afraid to let them in.

You can meditate, set an intention. What do you want to discover? You don't have to do this every time you meditate—most of the time, you should just venture into the unknown. However, every once in a while, you can set an intention for yourself when you want to do deep work. You can simply ask yourself a question ahead of time. What do I need to know that I'm not seeing right now—to make a choice or simply live more fully? When you reach the deep meditative state, you can open your eyes, grab your journal, and start writing. Just let it flow. You can draw, make lists. Whatever just flows naturally from within, just let it come out.

While you can immediately examine what you wrote, you can also wait and go back after a few days, after you've let things sit. Then you can explore your words. Are there any patterns in your thoughts? Do you find yourself writing about certain things—fear or love? Are things chaotic or organized? As you begin to pick things apart, you will soon be able to piece things back together in a whole new way. The kaleidoscope—taking all the broken pieces of yourself, putting them all back together, and perceiving the beautiful soul that emerges. This is the moment of bliss.

OBSERVERS

Are some of us just here to observe? Like silent watchers, our role is perhaps to observe all that passes on the planet. The pain and darkness. The love and light. We wonder how humans can behave that way toward each other. How can God exist when there is so much suffering in the world? God is love and love is available to everyone. The suffering on our planet is not caused by God—it's caused by *us*. We are the cause of all the suffering. Humans are the ones that hurt each other—desiring power, wealth, and control. We ask God to intervene. Perhaps God can't intervene. We are here to learn lessons, grow, and evolve as spiritual souls. Hopefully, we can do this in our lifetimes. Hope is important. But we cannot blame a divine being for our problems.

So much in our world is gloriously beautiful, and it diminishes the darkness. Some live in worlds with equal measure of pain and love. Some are completely enveloped in darkness, sometimes through no fault of their own. Some choose the darkness, sealed shut, trapped, while others appear to flow smoothly through life, with grace and fluidity. Is this fate or choice? Do we have free will? Can we change the world?

Once we all awaken and recognize that we have the power to initiate change, then change will come. We are not helpless, at the mercy of anyone or any being. We can choose kindness, compassion, and love through our words and actions. We can help each other grow and evolve. We can lessen our desires for material gain. We control our destiny and that of humanity.

TRUST

Trust is complicated. Or is it? Either we trust or we don't. I don't believe you "sort of" trust someone. Either you believe someone or you don't. If you doubt someone's words, there's a lack of trust.

Sometimes we don't know we've been lied to. We continue skipping through life, naïve and unaware. Does it matter that we don't know?

Sometimes we know we've been lied to, but we don't say anything and try to let it go. Highly intuitive people often know when someone is lying. Sometimes we let "little white lies" go, but we still wonder *why there was even a need for a lie*, even a supposedly insignificant one. We nonetheless carry the burden and it affects our relationship. Does it matter that they don't know?

Sometimes someone confesses that they've lied. You're hurt, but at least you know the truth. Does it matter that everything is out in the open?

Every one of these examples impacts a relationship. Hidden or clearly visible, it impacts how you move forward with someone. Even if you don't know, it will affect your relationship. The other person carries the lie alone, and it changes their behavior. They must feel some sort of guilt. Or maybe not. There are those who don't seem to be fazed by lies.

There is no such thing as an insignificant lie. Any lie creates mistrust. How can you trust the other person again? How do you know if the small lie is the just beginning of more lies? If someone finds it so easy to lie to you, perhaps this is the beginning of more, as we head down a slippery slope of truth.

I suppose it's all personal. Some people are willing to accept little lies as if they are unimportant. Some people are willing to tell little lies as if they are unimportant.

But why lie? People who don't share the truth are not really trying to protect your feelings, but protecting themselves. It's a two-sided thing, trust. When it's broken, both parties suffer. The one who broke the trust feels guilt…the one who was deceived feels pain. If it's to be repaired, you need to rebuild the trust.

How do we rebuild that trust, so we can continue a relationship that once seemed so beautiful? We wonder if the entire relationship is a lie.

For some who have had their trust broken numerous times, it's difficult to repair a relationship where lies, or even a single lie, occurred. We need to figure out how to trust again. Whether it's in that relationship or a new one, it requires open communication. If you can work through the reasons behind the lie, understand exactly what happened, and forgive, it can be repaired. If not, as you move forward, you will need to find a way to trust again.

While you can lay blame on the other for their lie, if you want to repair things, it's important to understand the reasons behind the lie. Some lies are blatant and planned, hiding some sort of betrayal, others are just something that was said out of fear. You also must be willing to forgive. Otherwise, the resentment always becomes entwined in the relationship. Without honesty, forgiveness, and trust, the relationship is set for failure.

HOPE

Some say hope is dangerous, especially false hope. Don't believe it.

There is no false hope. Hope is hope, and it's necessary. It's never false. There is, however, a fine line between hope and expectations. We can hope and then release the expectations of whatever we envision. This is the ultimate surrender—surrendering to the Universe, allowing what is meant for us to enter. Not pinning our hope on specific people or desires but on overall blessings of love and beauty. A life of joy and meaning.

If we lose hope, how do we continue living? Hoping for love is real and positive. Expecting love is entirely different. If the Universe brings you things that are for your highest good, even if they are negative, it does not make hope irrelevant. You learn through the challenges. It's about exuding positivity and love, and in the process, drawing more positivity into your life. If things feel hopeless, if you are always in negativity, you'll just continue in a deep cycle of hopelessness, living in pain.

Expecting someone to love you is pointless. But you can hope for beautiful love. Release your expectations. Live life and don't dwell on your desires. If you expect someone to love you, someone who may not want to love you, you set yourself up for pain. You can hope, then let it go and enjoy your life. If they love you, they will find you. And if they don't, there will be someone else who comes along, even more amazing than the person who couldn't love you. Expectations create desperation, and living in desperation is a miserable way to live.

I've learned that hope is necessary, but we can't let expectations consume us. We venture into the realm of unrealistic desires once we get consumed by expectations. The death of a relationship may feel like the death of hope, and that's why it's so hard to let go. For me, I didn't want to feel hopeless. I lived my life with positivity, full of hope for the future. Giving up hope felt like giving up everything that was ingrained in my very being. Without hope—for love, for peace, for deep connections—our soul suffers. If we cease our expectations, what we imagine will happen, the happily-ever-after we concoct in our heads, and hold on to hope for a beautiful future and deeply connected love, we are on a path that eventually will bring amazing things our way.

Release your expectations. Have hope for abundance and love.

IMPERFECTION

The saying, *Nobody is perfect*, is true. I am not perfect. We are all imperfect souls, living lives of constant struggle for perfection. We may not speak that goal aloud—the goal of perfection—but that's where most of our struggles are born. We come into the world and already people expect things from us. Our parents, and eventually our friends, spouses, and bosses—and the cycle continues.

Sometimes people expect us to behave a certain way—usually what they believe to be the "right" way—so they try molding us into an acceptable image. This is where it all starts. We feel the pressure without even realizing where it's coming from. We must be kind, thoughtful, always respectful, and always well-behaved. And those are amazing qualities. But we all fail sometimes. We all flounder, as we learn and grow. Sometimes we unintentionally hurt others. Sometimes we're punished for it, either visibly or passively. We begin to strive to become better people. The pressure is on.

We are judged harshly for our mistakes at times, judged by an increasingly harsh society. With social media and our hyperconnected world, everything is out in the open. Every small transgression has become an unforgivable sin. Forgiveness is necessary, as is compassion and understanding, but so many want what they believe is justice, proclaiming judgment is a necessary part of society. Standards are set. We must be perfect mothers, fathers, and employees. Harsh punishment, unrelenting judgments.

No wonder we struggle. No wonder we suffer from a lack of self-love. How can we love ourselves when the world judges us so harshly and expects so much from us?

AUTHENTICITY

Be authentic. That's one of the best pieces of advice I ever received. Hard to get there though. You have to know who you are to be who you are. *Who am I?* A question many of us ask ourselves. Am I a mother? Doctor? Writer? You need to look beyond the labels assigned to you and by you. Those labels don't define who you are completely. You are more than that. You are nature. Love. Sunsets. Creativity. Just think about what you love to do. What are your qualities? What are your imperfections? Those are all the parts of you that define the "Who am I?" Similar to the "I am," those are the phrases that clearly define you in a world beyond the physical.

Sometimes it takes being beaten—reaching a point where you don't feel authentic at all—to understand what it means to be authentic. Sometimes we feel we have let down those who had admired us, looked up to us, wanted to learn from us. *I'm sorry I wasted your time.* At some point, we have to start over again. Remember, nobody has been let down, not others, not you. It's all part of the growth process. When you realize you are not authentic, that's when you move toward authenticity.

What does it mean to be authentic? Saying what you think and feel, even if others disagree with you or you ruffle a few feathers. Embracing your imperfections, loving them as much as the other aspects of yourself you love and already find beautiful. Being comfortable in your own skin, loving your body and all of its little idiosyncrasies. Not letting yourself be molded by society or others into something you are not. Not a phony, not a fake. Letting your hair go gray if you want. Ignoring the words of those who call you crazy or irresponsible. Living your life the way you desire and following your distinctive path, without fear of judgment.

UNCONDITIONAL LOVE

*W*hat is love anyway? It can't be defined by the mind or by science. We each have our definition of love. Love is personal. Is romantic love, the deep soul connections that come along every so often, really as rare as we believe? Those are the connections that change our lives and profoundly affect our souls. Some people never experience that kind of love. It's not because it's rare, but because we are often too blind to see when a deep soul connection comes our way. We are fearful, we are closed, we are living in ego and too connected to the material world. We have chosen the beige path. Safe and protected from harm.

When we allow ourselves to surrender—to love with vulnerability, allow love into our hearts—without expectations, love will find us. If we allow love to transform us, coloring our lives with prismatic hues, we live a fuller, more joyful life.

Love is the fusion of two souls who are drawn to each other. Not by chance, but by destiny. Perhaps they have been led toward each other their entire lives, slowly easing into union at the right moment. Those profound connections that make you feel as if you are home. When you meet, you may feel you already know this person—you instantly recognize their energy. You can feel each other without touching. You know what the other is thinking, and you speak the same words in unison. It's mystical and magical and you may wonder if it's real. You are so deeply connected that you are in moments fused into one. Looking into each other's eyes and truly sensing the other's soul. Knowing you are meant to be together and that you don't want to be apart. There's no judgment. Only acceptance of all their imperfections. This is unconditional love.

SURRENDER

*Surrender to the flow of life and you will find yourself
floating effortlessly in the river of grace.
~ Deepak Chopra*

A long, long time ago (okay, maybe not that long ago), I would make plans (work, fun, travel, food...anything) and if they didn't happen the way I had envisioned, a very clear vision that I had daydreamed in my mind, I would not be the happiest person. Annoyed, frustrated, worried...inflexible.

These were sometimes little things that some people would just easily shrug off. Changes to appointments, sudden unexpected arrivals. I recovered quickly, but those moments of, "BTW, we had to change the date of blah blah blah..." would throw me off balance. I would feel resentment toward others. *How dare you change my plans? My vision.*

My excuse was that I had created this vision, and it upset me because I had to recalibrate and come up with a whole new "story." Which was partially true.

What it was really about was control. I wanted to be in control of things, my life, my future. The thought that another's actions could impact me was slightly disturbing. *Nobody, nothing can take me away from my mission!* Whatever the mission was at that moment in time.

However, as we know, we have very little control over things outside of ourselves, and the more we try to fix things, find solutions, and make things happen the way we want and expect, the worse those things sometimes become and perhaps the worse we feel about not having control.

Surrendering is hard. But we don't have a choice. We can either spend our lives desperately and futilely trying to control everything, or we can surrender and allow ourselves to flow through life. Yes, there will be tough times and it's not smooth sailing over calm waters all the time. Life ebbs and flows. But at least we will release some of our desperation and pain...because we only cause ourselves more pain by believing we can control everything.

Fear of surrender is probably why the writer in me developed. As a writer, I can create my own story. I have total control, it all comes from my intuition. As a writer, I create worlds to learn from—beautiful worlds, difficult worlds—but in those worlds, I learn and grow and nobody can come in and change my story.

I learn and heal through creating. I write to learn more about myself, understand my fears and emotions, and then move through the healing process. That's why I love teaching my intuitive writing workshops. I'm teaching others how to get in touch with their intuition and discover who they are—the beautiful and the imperfect. That's how you move through healing. Knowing and accepting. Then eventually surrender.

Release the expectations of how you believe something *should* be. Flow through life. Instead of struggling in the weeds—hope and dream. And then release your expectations, needs, and desires to the Universe. Let it do its magic. And as you learn to live in the present moment, gratefully enjoying the small things, you will eventually stop trying to control situations and people. This flow brings you closer to balance so that you can enjoy the beauty of life and experience the love of self and others. Your pain and fear will transform into blossoms of love.

It's not easy and no human can ever be in the surrender and flow mode 100% of the time. We're all imperfect and beautiful. And that's how it should be in our flourishing gardens, free of the weeds that hold back our growth. We can continue to reach our arms to the stars, to the Universe, and allow ourselves to be free of the weeds that keep us stuck in an unkempt garden. As you look around your garden and see all the beautiful growth, surrender to the Universe. Everything that is meant for you will come in divine timing. And usually when you least expect it.

COMING SOON

THE WOMAN WHO EXHALED MIRACLES

She didn't realize what she was doing. She would just simply breathe. A normal inhale and long exhale. It was all ordinary. Just a life-sustaining pattern, a necessity for every creature—inhale the fresh air, exhale the stale air. The difference was that when the fresh air entered her mouth, it went through her entire body. It wound through every cell and molecule, and miraculously, right into her soul. There, where there was potent love and light and energy, the air changed. By the time the breath escaped, through her lingering exhale, it was infused with magical particles.

The particles found themselves in a realm without magic. They knew they couldn't survive without transformation, so they built an invisible world inside this new realm where anything was possible.

She continued to breathe, in and out, each time streaming more magical molecules into the air. A man would walk by and wish for love. Shortly after, love came into his life—a unique woman, rare, and unlikely to exist anywhere else except in his imagination. A girl walked by and wished for a pink hat, and the next day, her father came home from a business trip with a frilly pink hat, exactly as she had pictured it. An old woman wished for her husband, long bedridden by a severe illness, to heal and be able to take long walks with her again. Miraculously, the man improved and was soon seen walking with the woman in the park.

All the while, the woman was oblivious to the miracles. She simply lived her life, not believing in anything. Just breathing and remembering lost love, the pain of the past, and how she would be alone for the rest of her life. She didn't want to try again. There was too much pain in love, and she felt her soulmate perhaps hadn't even been born. She had come to terms with everything. She believed her true joy would be found in solitude. Experiencing adventures, having lovers with little or no emotional attachment. She accepted her fate. Love was not meant for her in this lifetime.

One day she met a strange, but likable, old woman. The woman offered to read her palm. She didn't want to know anything about her future, plus she believed the future was unpredictable, always malleable by free will. Except for hers. Her future was solitude. She made the choice—there was no universal power that could make that choice for her, and she felt in her heart that it was her only option.

"It's free!" the old woman cackled.

Nothing is ever free, she thought.

She asked the old woman, "Why?"

The old woman laughed again.

"Because it's time," the woman answered.

She thought about timing. Time was irrelevant to her. She would continue with her transitory life until death, when then, she would be taken to the light and be free of all her human pain. At least that's what she hoped. She once believed in a magical afterlife and hoped for love and freedom at the end of her life. But now, she wasn't so sure what would happen. No matter where she went or how she died, she would be free. She didn't need to know anything else.

Reticently, she agreed, holding out her hand for the woman.

The woman cackled again, taking her hand, and pulling it close to her face.

"I knew it! said the old woman, "It's you!"

"Me? What are you talking about? Who is "You?" she asked.

"You see this mark here," said the old woman, pointing to an infinity-shaped symbol on her palm.

Strange. She hadn't seen it there before.

www.ingramcontent.com/pod-product-compliance
Lightning Source LLC
Chambersburg PA
CBHW060604080526
44585CB00013B/680